LORD, INCREASE ME TODAY

LORD, INCREASE ME TODAY

17 Principles for Increase to Guarantee a Better Life.

ANTHONY J. CLARK

ISBN-13: 9780692629512
ISBN-10: 0692629513

This book is dedicated to my Lord and Savior Jesus Christ.

TABLE OF CONTENTS

INTRODUCTION

THANK YOU FOR choosing to read this book on increase. We all want to find a way to get better in life. On a daily basis, so many of us struggle with getting our lives on the right path for success. This happens many times because we try to do everything ourselves. Other times this happens because we choose to not trust God fully in all areas of our lives. This book will help you get on the right path that God intended for you to be on, and allow you to live your best life.

These 17 principles will help you to see all that God wants for you. Since you are reading this book, God has chosen you to be that difference maker in your family. In order for you to receive it, you have to believe fully that God is in control and that he will never lead you down a path of disappointment and heartache. Be sure to listen to the still, small voice inside of you. As you began to read this book, write down all of your thoughts that trigger you to make an adjustment. Prioritize those thoughts and go back and study that particular area. The scriptures throughout this book will also help you become stronger and closer to God. You are on your way to Increase and a better life!

INCREASE MY FAITH

I T IS ALL about believing. The definition of faith is complete trust or confidence in someone or something. Let us build on this for this entire chapter. We sometime have a hard time believing in things. Usually, if it is something that we have not actually seen for ourselves, we will not put too much credibility into it. Some of you are going through circumstances that your faith is small or even nonexistent. Christ wants us to start off by having just a little faith in him. Matthew 17:20 says, "He replied, because you have so little faith. I tell you the truth, if you have faith as small as a mustard seed, you can say to this mountain, 'Move from here to there' and it will move. Nothing will be impossible for you." We have so much power, but some of us do not know it. It starts with our beliefs. Remember that faith is complete trust or confidence in someone or something. Complete confidence!! God is the only someone that we can have complete confidence that he will deliver on what we ask for. Every human being that we come across cannot guarantee that they will never let us down. That is not humanly possible. We all fall short. However, I have seen when I am obedient and have faith in what God does, he delivers.

So let me give you a blueprint for the steps that you need to follow to build your faith.

Step 1, it starts with believing in Jesus. Romans 10:9-10 states, "That if you confess with your mouth, "Jesus is Lord," and believe in your heart that God raised him from the dead, you will be saved. For it is with your heart that you believe and are justified, and it is with your mouth that you confess and are saved." How important is verse 10? Many of us have heard Romans 10:9, but verse 10 gives a full understanding. With your heart you believe and are justified. It starts with our heart. God examines your heart first to see if you are truly real about your walk or if you are playing games. The great thing is that you can fool people, and sometimes even yourself; however, you cannot fool God. Confess with your mouth that you believe that Jesus died on the cross for your sins, and rose on the third day. If you do not know the Lord and you are ready, repeat out loud this prayer of salvation:

Lord Jesus, I believe that you died on the cross for my sins, and on the third day you rose from the dead. Forgive me for my sins. Come into my heart. I accept you as my Lord and Savior. I shall not die, but have eternal life.

Since you just said the prayer of Salvation, and believed in your heart that Jesus is Lord: **CONGRATULATIONS!!!!! WELCOME TO THE FAMILY OF BELIEVERS!!!!**

Eternal Life? Yes, eternal life. John 3:16 says, "For God so loved the world, that he gave his only begotten Son. That whosoever believeth in him shall not perish, but shall have eternal life." This is what it is all about. You have to believe in Jesus dying for everyone on the cross so you may have the opportunity for eternal life. Who does not want to live forever? I know I do. That is why I gave my life to Christ because I wanted more out of this life than just being a slave to sin. Once you give your life to Christ, you do not have to be a slave to the sins of this world.

Step 2 In the process of building your faith you have to be born again. John 3:3-6 states, "Jesus replied, Very truly I tell you, no one can see the kingdom of God unless they are born again." "How can someone be born when they are old?" Nicodemus asked. "Surely they cannot enter a second time into their mother's womb to be born!" Jesus answered, "Very truly I tell you, no one can enter the kingdom of God unless they are born of water and the Spirit. Flesh gives birth to flesh, but the Spirit gives birth to spirit." Once you are born again in the spirit, you are making a transformation of your mind and heart to follow Jesus.

Step 3 Now we have to change from our old ways of practicing in sin. 2 Corinthians 5:17 states, "Therefore if anyone is in Christ, the new creation has come. The old has gone, the new is here!" You have to let go of that old you that was out there living of the world. So what do I mean by practicing sin? When we are spiritually connected with Christ, we sometimes commit sin and not even know it. Remember, we all fall short of the glory of God. Ecclesiastes 7:20 says, "Surely there is not a righteous man on earth who does good and never sins." So sin does happen. However, practicing in sin means you are out there committing a sin like adultery and know that it is wrong, but you do not care. You are out there stealing money and committing other horrific acts, and you are not even trying to turn away from your evil ways. Because of our sins, we all would deserve death. However, because of grace and mercy we are given a second chance. Grace is defined as free and unmerited favor of God, as manifested in the salvation of sinners and the bestowal of blessings. The definition of mercy is compassion or forgiveness shown toward someone whom it is within one's power to punish or harm. Grace and mercy are best demonstrated in the salvation that is obtainable through Jesus Christ. We warrant sentencing, but if we accept Jesus Christ as Savior, we obtain mercy from God and we are set free from judgment. Instead of the verdict of death, we obtain by grace forgiveness of sins, abundant living, and salvation. Understand that grace wants to come across you. Grace wants to find us, and bless us. God has said that his grace is sufficient for us. We are protected by grace. However, we do not need to try and use this for an excuse to mess up, or disregard the law of the Old Testament. John 14:23 says, "Jesus replied, "Anyone who loves me will obey my teaching. My Father will love them, and we will come to them and make our home with them." If you love God with all your heart, and your soul, and your entire mind, you love the law of the Old Testament too. There are many lessons being taught on grace and I will not go into a lesson, but just understand that grace will protect you, but do not abuse it.

Step 4 This is a challenging step that we have to constantly remind ourselves of who and who's we are. We need to walk by faith and not by sight. 2 Corinthians 5:7 says, "For we live by faith, not by sight." As Christians, we should not be living by the things that we can see in front of us. What I mean by this is your circumstances may not be the best at this time, but having faith in God will turn it around. I have struggled in my finances for many years. However, since I have been walking by faith and not by sight, God has turned my finances around. I have gradually seen God turn it around because of my faith and obedience. When I could not see a way, I held on to my faith. Mathematically and scientifically there was no way for my finances to get better, but having hope and believing that Jesus is still in control turned it around. The doctor may tell you some bad news about your health, but you are not trusting in man. God controls the medical staff and the report. When you have faith in him, it does something special to God. What we show him is that no matter what man says I am trusting in you Jesus!! When you have strong and persistent faith, God will show up and show out!!!

So now that we have moved into another level of faith, let me bring this next point home that can separate the men from the boys or the women from the girls!! Faith without works is dead. I am going to show you in James 2: 14-24, and break these versus down for you. James 2: 14-24 says, "What does it profit, my brethren, if someone says he has faith but does not have works? Can faith save him? If a brother or sister is naked and destitute of daily food, and one of you says to them, "Depart in Peace, be warmed and filled," but you do not give them the things which are needed for the body, what does it profit? Thus also faith by itself, if it does not have works, is dead. But someone will say, "You have faith, and I have works." Show me your faith without your works, and I will show you my faith by my works. You believe that there is one God. You do well. Even the demons believe- and tremble! But do you want to know, O foolish man, that faith without works is dead? Was not Abraham our father justified by works when he offered Isaac his son on the altar? Do you see that faith was working together with his works, and by works faith was made perfect? And the Scripture was fulfilled which says, "Abraham believed God, and it was accounted to him for righteousness." And he was called the friend of God. You see then that a man is justified by works, and not by faith only." I was taught early in my Christian walk that all you need is faith. That was someone just telling me that information, but I had never read it for myself.

Let us understand that Abraham was counted righteous because he believed. He believed everything that God had told him about being the father of all nations. The point that James Chapter 2 is making in reference to Abraham's faith is the act of him making the attempt to sacrifice his son Isaac was essentially the work acting out from his faith that God was going to deliver on his promise no matter what. Abraham understood that the situation was bigger than him and Isaac. He understood that if he had to put his son on the Altar to become the father of all nations than he was willing to sacrifice one close to him to fulfill the promise of many. I went to church and heard a Pastor preaching on punching your timecard. His message was basically saying that when we go to work we make sure we punch that timecard so we can get paid on payday. If we do not punch it we will not get paid. It is the same when we activate our faith with works. When we are serving others, when we are volunteering to help someone on our off time, when we are doing a good deed for a stranger, when we are attending Bible study, and when we are ushering or working in the church we are punching our timecard for Jesus. We cannot just go around saying that we have faith, but we are not acting on it. If we are just sitting around not trying to find our fit in the church, we are having faith without works. You have heard the saying, "actions speak louder than words." Ask yourself; when was the last time I punched my timecard for Christ? If it has been a while you need to get busy and start serving the Lord everyday by reading the word, praying and praising him daily, and helping others as often as the opportunity comes up.

When we believe in things that we cannot yet see, that is faith. Hebrews 11:1says, "Now faith is being sure of what we hope for and certain of what we do not see." Do not let yourself get caught up in the things you see in this world, and start believing and trusting in material things. We have to work on self denial. Do not put yourself first, but learn how to put God first. Walk with the Lord in faith and see him exalt you and elevate you. Understand that when God sees that you are obedient, and have full trust, love and confidence in him with no doubt, he will start to gradually turn everything around for you. Your faith is worth more than anything to God. 1Peter 1:7 states, "These have come so that your faith of greater worth than gold, which perishes even though refined by fire may be proved genuine and may result in praise, glory and honor when Jesus Christ is revealed." Even though gold is refined by fire, it still perishes. However, your faith is eternal. God promised to supply all of our needs. All the extra stuff that we ask for is not mandatory for God to give to us. When we are obedient and trust in him to give us the desires of our hearts, and we are walking out in faith, we can ask God for gigantic prayers. When those prayers are lined up with God's plan for you, they will get delivered! It may not be in God's plan for you to win the Lottery. He knows that if you win, someone may do harm to you or you may not do the right thing with it, and may turn to money as your new God. God wants to get all of the glory. We are his creation, and he does not want anyone to take credit for your success but him. Honor him with your faith daily and tell him how much you appreciate him and what he does and has done for you.

One last point I want to hammer home about faith. We all know the story in Exodus where the people of Israel was trying to cross over into the promise land. However, it took them forty years to get there! Why did it take them so long? They were complaining about everything. God gave the children of Israel manna to eat every day for forty years. Think of Manna as a pancake. It appeared on the ground each day as flakes. They simply had to ground it like grain. This was after God delivered them from Egypt where they were slaves. He was supplying their needs. What did they do? They started complaining about they did not have any meat! God even dropped quail out of the sky in the evening for them, and they still complained. They wanted to go back to Egypt because they did not want to have to think about their next meal. Whenever things got a little uncomfortable, they wanted to give up. Can you imagine! Suppose you have a close friend that has just been set free from prison, and now you are going to bring them some free food every day until they can get back on their feet. However, your friend says, "I do not have any bacon with my pancakes! When I was in prison that is what we had. I rather go back because I was getting fed!"

How about the trip to the promise land? I read that the trip should have only taken 10 days. I also read that walking around the mountain was approximately a half mile. However, it took them 40 years because of their uprising and breaking of the rules. They were not satisfied by anything God was doing because they wanted things another way. Doesn't that sound like us today? We become disobedient and start grumbling about everything, and want God to bless us. That is not how it works. Prove yourself worthy by trusting him and he will come through for you.

The bottom line is that the Israelites lacked faith. They were not willing to trust that God had everything under control. God is faithful and will supply all of our needs. He had everything under control, it just was not moving fast enough for them. The manna stayed brand new so long as the people followed his guidelines. God even made water come out of a rock for them!! The Israelites shoes and clothing did not wear out for 40 years because God made sure of it.

So how do we increase our faith? Stop worrying and complaining about the things that you think you are lacking. God knows what we need before we ask for it. Will we make mistakes? Of course we will. We have to repent of our sins to make it right with God. Forgiveness from God will come through repentance. You can increase your faith by following Matthew 6:33. It says, "But seek first the kingdom of God and his righteousness, and all these things will be added to you." God wants us to seek those riches through Christ Jesus. Philippians 4:19 says, "And my God will supply every need of yours according to his riches in glory in Christ Jesus." Remember, the definition of faith is complete trust or confidence in someone or something. We have to show complete trust and confidence in Jesus Christ. Pray to him and surrender yourself to him. I want you to pray this prayer:

Lord I cannot do this on my own. I trust you Lord, and I want you to guide my steps. John 15:7 says, "If you abide in me, and my words abide in you, you shall ask what you will, and it shall be given unto you." I am going to be obedient and not grumble and complain when life becomes a little uncomfortable. I will trust in you and become an empty vessel that you can use to advance the kingdom of God. In Jesus name, Amen

INCREASE MY BOLDNESS

WHAT DOES IT mean to be bold to you? For me being bold use to mean that I had to prove myself to people in a macho way. I was wrong with my behavior and culture of what boldness is. The definition of boldness is not hesitating or fearful in the face of actual or possible danger or rebuff; courageous and daring. God wants us to live boldly and carry out our daily lives in his name. Hebrews 4:16 says, "Let us therefore come boldly unto the throne of grace, that we may obtain mercy and find grace to help in time of need." Growing up as a young man in the inner city of Philadelphia, I was always taught to respect my elders, and only talk when I was spoken to. This hindered my ability at times to be more outspoken, and to speak out in front of large groups of people.

It was not until I joined the United States Army that I was forced to speak in front of a captured audience. I would always ask God to give me the courage to say the right things. On one occasion I was in a military leadership school, and had to give a class on a topic that I had no prior knowledge of. When I stood up in front of my peers to give the presentation, I stood there with my hands behind my back (the position of parade rest for my veteran readers) and spoke unsure of myself. I was embarrassed and knew that I needed to get better in order to improve my public speaking skills. With plenty of repetition over the years, I have grown to be comfortable with both public speaking and giving presentations. That helped me with my boldness, but it was not everything I needed to increase this principle.

There are several examples in the Bible about boldness. However, the story about David in my opinion is probably the most inspirational. David was not as big as his brothers, but he was a man after God's own heart. He went up against

Goliath, and defeated the giant because of his boldness. This boldness was something that God put down inside of him because of his desire to seek after the Lord. Matthew 6:33 says, "But seek first his kingdom and his righteousness, and all these things will be given to you as well." To seek first his kingdom and his righteousness means to turn to God first for help, to fill your thoughts with his desires, to take his character for your pattern, and to serve and obey him in everything. What is a priority for you? Money, relationships, careers, sporting events, etc…all compete for the number one spot in our lives. However, we have to actively choose to make God our first priority in everything that we do.

Putting God first is the key to increasing our boldness. God would rather we come to him boldly asking for the desires of our hearts, than to come weeping in pain asking for the things we want. We develop our boldness with God by keeping a constant relationship with him. We need to talk to him daily as often as possible. Look at your relationship with your heavenly Father similar to your parents here on earth.

Most of us will talk to our parents and spend time with them daily when we are living with them. We ask them for all of our wants and desires, and expect them to make it happen for us. When we come to our parents asking them for our wants, do we come to them unsure of what to ask for? Do we come to them with a faint voice? No, we come to them with what we want and assume that it will be done. This is how we should approach our Heavenly Father with this type of boldness. We should daily come to God boldly asking him for huge prayers. We should ask him for things that are not within our natural grasp. We should boldly ask for things that in the natural may seem impossible, but through God all things are possible.

In 2014, my nine year old son put his Christmas list together in November. I saw him typing it up on the laptop, but I just thought how advanced elementary schools are these days with PowerPoint presentations! When he finally brought the list to me I was surprised to see the total price of $860. Can you imagine? A nine year old asking for items from specific stores and a total that was over the top for his age. That was an act of boldness. I must admit that I was surprised, but I did see him get more courage to ask for more this year than the year before. He knew that he had been obedient, and he had faith that he could ask for more. This is how God wants us to come boldly to the throne, and think big for our dreams. James 4:3 says, "When you ask, you do not receive because you ask with wrong motives, that you may spend what you get on your pleasures." I realize through this Bible verse and some of life's experiences, that God wants us to ask for things that will glorify the kingdom of God. I like to call this Kingdom business! When the things you are coming boldly to the throne for is lined up with Kingdom business, God will honor it.

Another form of boldness is simply doing the right thing. I know we have all heard the cliché taking the path of the hard right over the easy wrong. This takes boldness because the masses will more than likely take pleasure over discipline. I know a man that had to make a tough choice. His best friend was discriminating against minority employees. This man went to his friend and told him that this was not right, and he could not continue to sit back and look the other way. He lost his relationship with his best friend because he stood up for what was right. He told me that it hurt him a great deal to lose that friendship, but he did not lose sleep at night because he knew he did the right thing. God wants us to stand up for what is right no matter how difficult it may be. He does not want us to go into a shell and shrink when it comes to standing up to others for what is right. God wants us to be accountable for doing well any day of the week.

There is another element to boldness that many of us have a tendency to overlook. Learning to ignore certain situations is an act of boldness. When your co-worker or classmate gets under your skin, it is easy to want to give them a piece of your mind. However, Proverbs 12:16 says, "Fools show their annoyance at once, but the prudent overlook an insult." We have to learn that we cannot look to fight every battle. Sure we want to prove to people that our opinions matter, but the battle is not ours, it is the Lord's battle. I was on vacation with my wife once for our anniversary, and there were a few individuals that we could tell that were making statements looking to get a reaction from someone. Yes, it was annoying what they were doing, but I made up in my mind to ignore them because it was not worth my time to engage in a useless incident. How many times have we heard people say just walk away instead of getting in a fight or argument? This could keep plenty of men and women out of trouble if they could just be bold enough just to say, I am not going to let this still my joy. I am going to be a more mature person. Being bold is not always standing up to a situation. It is just as important to show your boldness by being able to walk away.

My final element to help you increase your boldness is being able to stand boldly for your beliefs and values. I know a gentlemen that works for a large organization, and his boss is a hard man to deal with. The company was having a Halloween party, and they were requiring all employees to participate. The gentlemen did not attend the party that evening because he does not believe in celebrating Halloween. The next day when he came to work the boss left word with the receptionist to let him know that he needed to see the boss as soon as he arrived. My friend became a little nervous. When he met with his boss, he asked him why he did not show up for this mandatory event. The gentlemen told him because of his spiritual belief he does not engaged in pagan holidays such as Halloween. He told me his boss eyes got big, and he began to turn apple red! There was a moment of silence. The next words out of his mouth may surprise you. The boss said to him, "I respect your candor and appreciate that you stand for something. It is about time we have someone around here that is not a yes man! We were looking to advertise an opening for a consultant position, but with your integrity and strong values, we have found who we need. Congratulations on your promotion!!" Wow. What a great story. When you boldly stand up for what you believe in, it can lead to God exalting you into positions you never thought you would get elevated to.

So what is the key to increasing your boldness? In order to increase your boldness you should keep God as your first priority in your life, be obedient to God, and have faith that he can do all things. Put these key factors into practice immediately and develop a relationship with God, and watch how things turn around for the better. I want you to also pray this prayer:

Lord you word says in Acts 4:31, "And when they had prayed, the place where they had gathered together was shaken, and they were all filled with the Holy Spirit, and began to speak of God with boldness." Lord give me the courage to conduct myself with enthusiasm to always stand up and do what is right. In Jesus Name, Amen

INCREASE MY OBEDIENCE

THIS CHAPTER IS one that we can all say that we have been guilty of doing our own thing at one time or another. The definition of obedience is compliance with an order, request, or law or submission to another's authority. Obedience is something that we struggle with. It is easy to want to go along with the masses to fit in and take the easy wrong instead of the hard right. As an Army Instructor at a high school teaching JROTC, I observe students daily following some of the misguided kids to be a part of the in crowd. Some students start off with such promise the first month of school. However, I begin to see who they are becoming by the November timeframe. That is when I have a tendency to have a mentor session with the cadet to get their attention and tell them what I see from the outside looking in. This is similar to what God does with us when we make our choices in life.

I have studied and realized that obedience is the first law of heaven. Matthew 22:37-40 states, "Jesus said unto him, Thou shalt love the Lord thy God with all thy heart, and with all thy soul, and with all thy mind. This is the first and great commandment. And the second is like unto it, Thou shalt love thy neighbor as thyself. On these two commandments hang all the law." As we already know that all the commandments are important. God wants us to be obedient and follow all of them. So how do we get there? This is a lifelong process. I look back and think about how my grandmother always wanted me to be in the house when the street lights came on, and I always seem to miss the timeframe. I was being disobedient to her, and I knew that it was wrong; however, I was having fun and did not want to give up the pleasure. It is similar to our relationship with God when it comes to obedience.

As adults, we all know the difference between right and wrong, but we do not want to give up our pleasures, addictions, etc… because we believe it makes us feel good and alive. The reality is that nothing comes out of being disobedience but heartache and pain. We can go for a while out of order with God, but eventually he will get our attention.

Ephesians 6:2-3 says, "Honor your father and mother which is the first commandment with a promise. "So that it may go well with you and that you may enjoy long life on the earth." Let us first break down the difference between honoring and obeying. When you honor someone, you love them and respect them. It does not mean that you have to agree with everything that they tell you and advise you on, but you do not have to belittle them or disrespect them. Children do not always honor their parents for many different reasons. Many of those reasons come down to children feeling that their parents are not doing enough for them. It may be the dad who is not there because his occupation causes him to travel frequently and the child feels abandoned. It could be the single parent that is trying to make ends meet by working two jobs. However, some children do not see things from that perspective. This is when they find a reason to lash out and dishonor their parents because they do not fully understand what the parent is going through. To obey means to do what you are told to do. Children are to first obey their parents while they are living under the roof that their parents provide for them. However, we should honor our parents for life.

Here's my testimony about my parents. I grew up in the inner city of Philadelphia, Pa. My mother lost her mother in an accident when she was 7 years old, and my uncle was just an infant. My mom's dad was an alcoholic, so she was raised by her aunt and my great grandmother. My mother was 14 years old when she had me. She was just a baby herself, and my dad was 20, as I thought. The grace and mercy of God was on her life to get her through a time when she had minimum guidance. When I was about 6, I had a choice on whether I wanted to live with my grandparents on my dad's side or live with my mom. I chose my grandparents because I thought that this was the place for me to be. My mom and my dad married and he joined the United States Marine Corps. I would see them from time to time, and when I was seven years old, my mom had my little brother. She named him Earl. Seventeen months after Earl was born, my mom welcomed another baby boy named Derrick. Everything seemed fine in Philadelphia, and my parents seemed happy with my brothers also. I spent time with my Uncle (my mother's brother) in Philly often. When he gave his life to Christ, he became a new person. One thing that he was about was integrity. I was talking to him one afternoon when I was thirteen, and I told him that my mom and dad were in Washington, D.C. and I was proud of them. Then, everything changed with his next words. He told me, "that man is not your daddy." I was so confused and devastated. I was being raised by my step grandparents and did not know it. My uncle told me he knew my father and he was going to contact him. I did not tell my step grandparents (from this point on I will refer to them as my grandparents) what was going on because I was not sure myself. I spoke to my biological father on the phone one day, and we scheduled for him to meet me at my school at the end of the school day. I waited for him, but he did not show up. I walked home very sad. I was sitting upstairs in my room when I heard the doorbell ring. My grandmother went to the door, but would not let the man that rung the doorbell in. She told him to go away and she did not know what business he had with me. When I came downstairs he was gone. She asked me over and over again while I sat there in tears, who was this man looking for me. I was reluctant to tell her, but after constant interrogation, I yelled out, "THAT WAS MY FATHER!!!" You could hear a pin drop in the house it was so quiet.

I got on the phone with my mother and asked her why she did not tell me about my father. She told me she was waiting until the right time to let me know. She also told me that she had not seen my father in years, and he may be dangerous. She told me how he had a girlfriend the same time he was dating her, and I had a sister born four months after me. My mother said my father married the lady he had a daughter by, and they lived in Yeadon, Pennsylvania. My relationship with my grandmother changed in my eyes at that point. I know that she still loved me, but it was not the same. I went to live with my mom when I was going into my junior year of high school. It humbled me because my mom was raising my two little brothers, and we did not have much. We slept on air mattresses and had minimum luxuries. I was not use to those living conditions when I lived with my grandparents who gave me everything. I was disobedient and disrespectful at times and was made to go back to Philly for my senior year. I ended up living with my Uncle for my last year of high school. During that time, my father knew that I was staying there because my Uncle told him, but he did not come and visit me. 13 years later I was in the United States Army stationed in Germany. I received a fatal call from my family in October 2000. My brother Earl was murdered. My mom still lived in the Maryland –D.C. area so I flew home on leave from Germany to help bury my brother. As you can imagine my family was devastated. My baby brother Derrick, and my brother who was murdered, Earl were so close because of the one year age difference. We buried my brother, and I went to Philly to spend time with the other side of my family. While I was in Philly, my uncle said that my biological father wanted to come and see me at my grandparent's house. This was the moment of truth. Finally, I was going to meet this guy that I was supposed to meet 17 years ago! The doorbell rang, and this time I answered the door. He came in and without hesitation; I gave him a big hug. I was especially interested in not only meeting him, but meeting my sister who was only 4 months younger than I. When we sat down and I asked about her, he told me that she was killed in a car accident on January 10, 1991. Her name was Tammy, and the news about her death saddened me. He told me that I had another sister and brother. My dad said he felt God was giving him a second chance with me because he was not on good terms with his other two children. However, let me tell you what was even more shocking. My cousin Kia and I are very close. When we were younger and she lived in another part of the city, I use to always go visit her when my grandparents took me out there. I told her over the phone that night I had met my dad, but my sister that was four months younger than I died in a car accident in 1991. However, I had a younger brother and sister. When I told her their names, she told me to stop what I was doing and come to her house. I went to her house, and she showed me a picture of my sister Tammy, and told me she was her best friend!! I asked, "Why didn't I ever meet her?" She told me that when I use to come over to visit, she would leave Tammy's house to come and play with me.

She knew my family the whole time, but did not know we were related. Had she took me outside with her, and my father would have tried to see me at my Uncle's house, I may have met my sister Tammy at that time. But I have to say, God has his purpose for everything.

In 2004, my younger brother Derrick was dealing with bi-polar disorder. He was in a deep depression from my brother Earl's death. In June 2004, my brother Derrick died by suicide. I came to bury him in Maryland, and again I went to Philadelphia to visit family. This time my dad introduced me to my little sister and brother. We have been close ever since.

So what was the point of telling you all of this? Well, it goes back to honoring you father and mother. After the age of 5, I only lived with my mother about two years of my life. I did not meet my father until the age of 30. I could have been upset and angry about how they did not raise me, but instead I understood the commandment of honor thy father and thy mother and your days will be long. I also understand that God put me in the household I grew up in for a reason. Through it all, I have been respectful and love both of my parents through the years. I understand that parents do not wake up wanting to not do the best for their kids. They generally are doing the best that they know how. We need to be obedient and respect that, so it can release us from heartache and pain we may experience for not giving our parents the benefit of the doubt.

It is especially difficult when you know the word of God, and you do not obey. 2 Peter 2:21 says that, "It would be better if they had never known the way to righteousness than to know it and then reject the command they were given to live a holy life." I have not always been obedient in many areas of life. However, the one that registers loudly in my mind is God telling us to tithe in church. I knew that I was supposed to bring my tithe (money) to the storehouse (church), and I would be blessed. Instead, I was in church for years and did not pay it. In 2013, the same position that I am in now was taken away from me. I was laid off because I was the third instructor in that position, and when the school made cuts I was the first to go. As I look back now, I do believe since I was not obedient to what the word of God says, he took a means of financial security away from me. He later restored me because of my obedience and he brought me back to my current position. However, I had to go through a season of financial difficulty to learn that God is in control.

Obedience brings blessings. Sure, we have had many people tell us that we are blessed even when we know we may be living a not so straight and narrow life. What we do not realize is that it is God's grace and mercy that allows good things to happen to us even when we are not living right. To get the fullness of what God wants to give us we have to become obedient. We have to remove the "I" nature, and get to a point that we are focused on putting God first and keeping his commandments. This is where we experience the true blessings of God. When we are obedient, God has no choice but to bless us. There are many areas in the Bible that talk about obedience. Deuteronomy 28 speaks specifically about obedience to the people of Israel. Verse 1 and 2 says, "If you fully obey the Lord your God and carefully follow all his commands I give you today, the Lord your God will set you high above all the nations on earth. All these blessings will come on you and accompany you if you obey the Lord your God." The entire 28th chapter of Deuteronomy teaches about what will happen with obedience, and starting at verse 15 it talks about what will happen if you are disobedient. Yes, this was God talking to the children of Israel, but it is still relevant today. Think about it!! Do you know of one child that has always been obedient and has done everything that their parents have instructed them to do? No. However, through Christ Jesus we get a second chance at being obedient to the word of God. 2 Corinthians 5:17 says, "Therefore, if anyone is in Christ, he is a new creation; old things have passed away; behold, all things have become new." This means that through Christ that the disobedience of the past before you gave your life to Jesus is forgiven and forgotten by God. From that point on you should make a conscience effort to walk in obedience. Will you be perfect? Of course not, and no one expects you to be perfect. You will make mistakes, but when we do we need to repent and move toward not constantly falling back into disobedient actions and behavior.

So how do we increase our obedience? We increase our obedience by having faith in God and doing the right thing in life and towards others. If we do not have faith in our relationship with God and know that God will deliver on his promise, then we will not grow. I want you to also pray this prayer:

Jesus, your word says in John 15:14 "If you love me, you will keep my commandments." Lord it is not about me, but it is all about you. Teach me Lord to be more obedient and receptive to your word. Give me desire and strength to read your word daily which is a step in the right direction. I want to be better and any unclean spirits that are trying to live in me or latch on to me so I can be disobedient, wash me clean!! In Jesus name, Amen.

Romans 10:17 says, "Faith comes by hearing the Word of God and responding in confident trust." Once we have the faith and confidence in Jesus, our obedience will increase amazingly.

INCREASE MY FINANCES

FINANCES ARE AN area that many people want to increase in. One definition of finance is the management of large amounts of money. There are plenty of get rich schemes out there that simply want to lure you in so that you can help them get rich. When I was younger, I had fallen victim to some of these infomercials, and always came up short. I invested in the stock market, but that is not consistent like we want it to be. I worked hard in the United States Army for 20 years, and managed to make it up through the ranks. However, whenever it seems I was taking three steps forward financially, something happened where I had to take 4 steps back. I can give you one method that will increase your finances which is the only guarantee in life when it comes to wealth. It is through tithes and offering. In Malachi 3:10 it states, "bring the whole tithe into the storehouse, that there may be food in my house. Test me in this," says the Lord Almighty, "and see if I will not throw open the floodgates of heaven and pour out so much blessing that there will not be room enough to store it." This is the only place in the Bible where God says to test him. Ladies and gentlemen; this works. The definition of tithe is one tenth of annual produce or earnings. I had not paid my tithes for years. I would go to church and give my ten or twenty dollar offering. God was blessing me, but I was not being obedient. If we expect to get God's excellence, we have to do our part by operating in excellence.

I started paying my tithes faithfully in March of 2014. My wife and I had tried everything else, but our finances were not going in the direction we expected it to go. I got laid off of my Army JROTC instructor position in June of 2013, but I had found a position at the Department of Veteran Affairs in

December 2013. I was making half the pay I was making at the school, but had the same bills. My wife and I sat down and figured how we could pay our tithes by getting together to help each other with bills. I know that in the Old Testament it says to pay ten percent of your earnings. However, 2 Corinthians 9:6-7 says, "the point is this: whoever sows sparingly will also reap sparingly, and whoever sows bountifully will also reap bountifully. Each one must give as he decided in his heart, not reluctantly or under compulsion, for God loves a cheerful giver." Many of us was raised and taught that the 10 percent rule for tithing is the only way. God wants us to give our best. Whatever our best may be, that is what you need to give. God knows your heart. I do want you to understand that when we set aside the 10 percent for your tithes, God makes that Holy. God blesses the other 90 percent of our money also. In the Bible, money is considered the root of all evil. The only way your money will be blessed is if God blesses it. If you never tithe, your money will continue to receive setbacks. My wife and I looked at our finances and decided we could give 10 percent. God has been blessing us financially ever since.

It does not stop there. Remember, I was making half the money I was making at the school. However, since I started paying my tithes consistently, my money seemed to be stretching and going further. I was not doing anything different except faithfully paying my tithes. I had been working at the Department of Veteran Affairs since December 2013. On August 4, 2014 I received an email from my old principal asking me if he could meet with me sometime that week. I told him that I could meet him on that day, but I would not get out to the school until around 5 pm. He wrote back and said I will see you then. I went out to the school to meet with him, and he offered me my old job back!! I was now the primary Army Instructor, and did not have to worry about being laid off this time. As a bonus, the new Senior Army Instructor is a Christian also, and we pray the day in together every morning! God restored me, and now I make double the money I made at the Department of Veteran Affairs. I will tell you that because of my consistency to pay my tithes in 2015, God blessed me with paying off all of my bills except my house!

I know now that all of this is because of my obedience in paying my tithes. I do want to point out that tithing is not just money. Tithing is also your time. Taking time to volunteer to help others out of the kindness of your heart is another form of tithing. Look at it like this; anything that you like, and are willing to give up to do God's will can be considered tithing. For example, instead of sitting at home on Saturday watching football all day, why not volunteer your time to become part of a prison ministry or go to a nursing home and witness to the elderly.

I want you to take notice of 2 Corinthians 9:7 when it talks about giving not grudgingly or out of necessity. God wants us to have a willing heart. God does not want us to feel forced into giving money to the kingdom. He wants us to be enthusiastic about our choice to give. Would you want someone to give you something, and give it to you with an attitude? I know I would not want to receive it.

When you do not pay God you are robbing God. Malachi 3:9 says, "You are under a curse- your whole nation- because you are robbing me." You may say why does it seem like every month something always comes up? The car breaks down. The car needs new tires, a new medical bill, etc... All these unnecessary financial situations seem to come up. That is because if you do not pay your tithes, God will get it back in another form. However, when you do pay it, God will bless you and will not allow those burdens to hit you constantly. I am not saying you will never have to replace your tires or have expenses come up, but when it does come God will provide a way for you when you are paying your tithes.

Another area of increasing your finances is giving to others. Luke 6:38 says, "Give and it will be given to you. A good measure, pressed down, shaken together and running over, will be poured into your lap. For with the measure you use, it will be measured to you." Giving your time and money to others will come back to you. Helping someone financially when the opportunity becomes available will always bring a smile to God. Tithes and offerings that you pay to the church are to help the church function, but to also help the poor, and it helps you! This is being a servant of God, and we should look for the opportunity to serve others always.

There is another point about finances that needs to be addressed. We are seeing more and more wealthy people go broke. It has never been more magnified than today. When you do not give back, God can take your possessions away. We all wonder why we cannot get ahead when we are not following God's will, and we seem to be stuck in a rut. Well here is the explanation. Proverbs 13:22 says, "The wealth of the sinner (finds its way eventually) into the hands of the righteous, for whom it was laid up." When we decide to trust in the Lord about our finances, money will run us down. This money is coming from those who are not following the word of God. The righteous will get their inheritance from God by it leaving the hands of those who do not put God as their first priority. When we pay our tithes, we are leaving an inheritance for our children and our tithes are being stored up in Heaven too. Ecclesiastes 2:26 says, "To the person who pleases him, God gives wisdom, knowledge and happiness, but to the sinner he gives the tasks of gathering and storing up wealth to hand it over to the ones who pleases We need to understand that when we are being obedient in our finances and having expectancy (along with living a righteous life) that our wealth will grow. Having faith that the best is yet to come, will thrust us further into our rightful inheritance from the Lord. God wants us to be consistent in our tithing and giving.

There are plenty of things that I have expressed about finances. However, I want to make sure I bring this point home. You cannot serve God and money. Matthew 6:19-24 says, "Do not store up for yourselves treasures on earth where moths and vermin destroy, and where thieves break in and steal. But store up for yourselves treasures in heaven, where moths and vermin do not destroy, and where thieves do not break in and steal. For where your treasure is, there your heart will be also. The eye is the lamp of the body. If your eyes are healthy, your whole body will be full of light. But if your eyes are unhealthy, your whole body will be full of darkness! No one can serve two masters. Either you will hate the one and love the other, or you will be devoted to the one and despise the other. You cannot serve both God and money." Remember, we can obtain things here in this world, but do not make it your focus. We should be seeking to complete God's purposes in all that we do, not simply what we do with our money. It is obvious that having the incorrect riches leads to our spirit and mind being in the wrong position. What we value the most runs us, whether we own up to it or not. If wealth or riches grow to be too significant to us, we must regain control or do away with these objects. The Lord demands for a choice that allows us to be in this world cheerfully with anything we have because we have selected eternal worth over short-term, earthly riches.

So how do you increase your finances? It can be so simple, but we make it hard. Give the tithe and offering to the church cheerfully, and God will open up opportunities for you. When you give your tithes in the form of money, do not pay them for the sole purpose of expecting something in return. Do it because you love God and you want to be obedient and honor him. I want you to also pray this prayer:

Lord your word says in Malachi 3:10 to bring the whole tithe into the storehouse, that there may be food in my house. Test me in this, "says the Lord Almighty, "and see if I will not throw open the floodgates of heaven and pour out so much blessing that there will not be room enough to store it." Lord, you said test you in this and I am trusting you, I am going to be obedient and pay my tithes this coming payday. Bless me Lord in my finances. In Jesus Name, Amen

We also have to believe that God can do exceedingly above and beyond what we can imagine. God is supernatural and he can give you whatever he wants to give you. God does not need your money. We do not have to tithe, we get to tithe!! God just wants to see how much you love him by being obedient. We have to trust in the Lord, and stop trying to control our finances. It will make life a whole lot simpler when it comes to money. Many people get money and wonder why they cannot sustain it over a lifetime. When you pay your tithes and put your faith in God, you will be able to maintain your finances. Remember, in order for God to bless all of our money, we have to pay the ten percent. Psalm 24:1 states, "The earth is the Lord's and the fullness thereof, the world and those who dwell therein." Since the Lord control's everything, why focus on material things? Keep God first priority in your life, and he will take your finances to a level that you cannot even imagine.

INCREASE MY ABUNDANCE AND PROSPERITY

LET US START off by studying the definition of abundance and prosperity. The definition of abundance is a very large quantity of something. The definition of prosperity is the state of being prosperous. Some of the synonyms that go along with prosperity are success, profitability, wealth, luxury, fortune, security, and the good life. At one point in my life, I was taught that God does not want Christians to have a lot of money and be prosperous because money is the root of all evil. However, when money is not your focus it can be used as a tool to do many good things for the Kingdom. God does not want us to lack for anything. John 10:10 says, "The thief comes only to steal and kill and destroy. I came that they may have life and have it abundantly." God wants us to live an abundant life.

There are a few things that we need to do to understand to get to a level of living in abundance. **First**, we have to know that we can live an abundant life. Romans 5:10 says, "For if while we were God's enemies, we were reconciled to him through the death of his Son, how much more, having been reconciled, shall we be saved through his life!" What this verse is saying is the love that made Christ depart this life is the same love that drives the Holy Spirit to exist in us and direct us daily. The power that lifted Christ from the dead is the same power that saved you and is accessible to you in your everyday life. **Second**, we have to realize that it is not about you. We pray to God thinking about only our own condition and things of this world that we want. We spend most of our time praying and seeking these things out in our-day-to day life. What we should be focused on is our Lord and Savior Jesus Christ, and how we can serve someone else. When we put him first, our abundance will come.

Third, we have to learn how to let go of the past. Our past will haunt us if we let it. When we give our life to Christ, we are born again. One of two things comes from living in the past. We are either glorifying our past and wish we were back there which brings back past memories of our life before we fully committed to Jesus, or we are haunted by our past and instead of leaving our worries there we develop a I am not good enough mindset. Neither one of these attitudes are good for our spiritual growth. Psalm 103:12 states, "As far as the East is from the west, so far has he removed our transgressions from us." Imagine being in an open field and looking as Far East, and then looking as far as you can to the West. Do you think that they will ever touch each other? No because East and West can never meet. This is the forgiveness that God has for us when we repent and he forgives us of our sins. He removes it from us and he forgets about it. So why should we stumble around in the past? We shouldn't; we should let it go and move forward.

The last thing is by no means let fear regulate your life. We have a tendency to let our insecurities and fears dictate why we cannot accomplish our dreams and goals. This is one of the primary things that hold us back in life. 2 Timothy 1:7 states, "For the Spirit God gave us does not make us timid, but gives us power, love and self-discipline. When the Holy Spirit lives inside of us we will feel confident through our daily walk and prayer about being capable of doing all things. Philippians 4:13 states "I can do all things through Christ Jesus who strengthens me."

God will empower you to do things that you never thought you were capable of doing. He will bring that gift that you have inside of you to the forefront. There are many examples of people that were behind the scenes, and God brought those individuals from the back to the front because of their trust in Jesus. When it is something great that you are going to do, God will make sure that you cannot do it by yourself because he wants to get all the glory. He will make sure the task is too big for you to complete on your own. You have to trust and believe and stay in a daily relationship with him, and he will guide you to victory.

So let us talk about prosperity. I told you early what the definition of prosperity is. You can have those luxurious things, but you cannot let those things have you. When God becomes the center of your universe, he will take care of the desires of your heart that is good for you. Notice I said what is good for you. Some things that we want to make us prosperous, God knows it will not be good for us. Remember, what may be good for one person may not be good for the next. We are all created unique, and everyone is different. Psalms 139:14 says, "I prays you because I am fearfully and wonderfully made; your works are wonderful, I know that full well." You are the only you out there! So do not compare what you have to someone else. We should always strive to do better because we should want to be a blessing for someone else. Hebrews 13:5-6 is one of my favorite verses when it talks about to getting caught up in things of this world. It says, "Keep your lives free from the love of money and be content with what you have, because God has said, "Never will I leave you; never will I forsake you. So we say with confidence, "The Lord is my helper; I will not be afraid. What can mere mortals do to me?" The key is to being content. Make every effort to live with less moderately, than craving for more. We should be happy with what we have instead of complaining about what we are missing. Do not put you trust and hopes in man when it comes to prosperity; put you hopes and trust in the Lord.

So how do you increase your abundance and prosperity? You increase your abundance and prosperity by trusting in God to supply all of your needs, and give you the desires of your heart. You do not need your mother, father, sister, brother, Uncle, Aunt, cousin, best friend, wife, husband, son, daughter, boss, co-workers, that big break from the job industry or entertainment industry, etc... ALL YOU NEED IS JESUS TO SUPPLY YOUR ABUNDANCE AND PROSPERITY. The sooner we realize that all we need is him, we can start to live a more abundant and prosperous life.

INCREASE MY KNOWLEDGE AND UNDERSTANDING

THE DEFINITION OF knowledge is facts, information, and skills acquired by a person through experience or education. The definition of understanding is the ability to comprehend something. When you want to increase your knowledge of a subject for college or learn how to fix things around the house, you read or take those classes. When we want to increase our knowledge and understanding of God, we need to read the Bible. The Bible (Basic Instructions before Leaving Earth) is the most effective book we can read to get better knowledge and understanding to what God wants us to do. This is where your knowledge and understanding for all things will start. I remember when I started working at the Department of Veteran Affairs as a Medical Support Assistant; I did not have any specific training for that position. I asked Jesus every morning to give me more knowledge, confidence and understanding to do a better job today than I did yesterday. Every day I gradually got better at the position. I believe that because I was praying that prayer daily that God answered my prayers. When we give it to God, he will work hard for us as long as we believe.

There is no excuse today to not pick up your Bible, and have some quiet time with God. Plenty of us have smart phones. There are so many Bible applications for the phone out there it is simply amazing! I have an app called the Bible in One Year. I wanted to read the bible from front to back for years. I had a hard back "one year bible" at one time, but the one I had did not go in chronological order. I understand that everyone is different when it comes to studying, and this method works for me the best. However, I was falling short because since it was not with me at all times, I did not crack it open until I was at home. Sometime I would try and get my reading in just before I fell asleep after a hard day at work!! I was not giving God my best. Now that I have the app on my phone, I can read everywhere. When I am on break at my job, I get a chance to read the word. Whenever I am waiting in the lobby at the dentist office, I get a chance to study the Bible. I am in the book of Acts now, and I will be finish reading the entire bible by January 14th of 2016 (I started reading from Exodus on January 14, 2015). I have gained so much knowledge and understanding by reading and studying the word of God. However, I know that I would not have gained the knowledge if I did not have the desire to start to study the Bible.

We have to also realize that when we read the word of God, that is God speaking to us. I use to believe that I was going to hear God speak to me in a normal voice. It wasn't until I started studying more that I realize that the Bible is a living word, and that God speaks directly to us through his word. Have you ever read something in the Bible, and went to church and the Pastor was speaking on something that you have just read? That is God speaking to us and giving us confirmation on what you have just read through the Bible.

Understanding can increase in several different ways. Simply just reading the word of God will not give you the knowledge and understanding you need to grow. We have to also study the word of God. One way is to attend a Bible study. This is where you can get a deeper understanding of what the Bible is saying. Sometimes when we study on our own, and we are not mature Christians, we will get confused in some areas of the Bible. Until I started attending Bible study, I was missing out on maturing in Christ. A good Bible Study class will challenge your knowledge, and the class should have homework weekly. Hopefully this homework is to study the next assignment within the New Testament, and discuss what you have learned from what you have studied throughout the week. This does a couple of things. This makes you get into the word, and it also enhances your knowledge of the Gospel of Jesus Christ. Don't get me wrong, the entire Bible should be studied, but there is something special about studying about Jesus that I cannot explain.

Another area that we can increase our knowledge and understanding is through inspirational books like the one you are reading. It helps when you read about issues that you have been through yourself and you can relate. When the book is inspired by the word of God, you should get a special feeling inside that makes you want to get more knowledge of who our Lord and Savior Jesus Christ is. I remember when I was a young man, and I use to watch the Philadelphia 76ers play on television. When the game was over, I wanted to go out and play like "Dr. J". I never accomplished that task! However, I was inspired not just by his basketball skills, but also by what the commentators were saying about his story and journey to the National Basketball Association. Their commentating gave me a broader knowledge of the game, and I understood the rules and how the different players acted and reacted to what was happening on the court. When we read different inspirational books, it can give us a different views of how being a Christian is special, and it can make us want to go out and do more. The Bible gives us a broader knowledge of the game of life, and allows us to read and understand what some of the different men and women went through in the Bible. Their stories are there so we can learn, and understand that if they went through difficult times and made it, we can too! The Bible has many great inspiring stories that can spark something in us all to make us want to be better.

God does not want us to try and figure everything out on our own. Proverbs 3:5 says, "Trust in the Lord with all your heart and lean not on your own understanding." What God is essentially saying here is do not put your trust and understanding in man. I know that I can absolutely say that everyone reading this book has had someone let them down at least once in their lives. When we lean on our own understanding, we put our whole burden on something or someone, trusting in them to make things happen for us. I know sometimes we feel that God does not always answer everything that we ask him to do. When we are trying to make decisions that are life changing, we feel like we cannot trust anyone. However, God knows what is best for us. We may feel like our decision is the best one, but God knows what is coming up around the corner. We need to understand that he is not going to lead us to a decision that will not work for our good. We must trust him in every decision that we make.

How do we increase our knowledge and understanding? Our knowledge and understanding comes from the Almighty God. We should not look to be approved by men, but we should seek to be approved by God. We have to be willing to give our thinking and decision making to God. We cannot be clever in our own eyes. We should at all times be eager to listen to and be approved by God's word and wise guidance. The way we increase our knowledge and understanding is to follow three steps. **First**, bring your decisions to God in prayer. Develop a relationship with God so that you can know when he is speaking back to you through confirmation of your prayers. **Second**, read the word and use it as direction. The Bible stands for Basic Instructions before leaving Earth, so while we are here we should be using it to guide us in our decisions and everything that we do. **Third**, follow God's direction. When we do these three things, our knowledge and understanding will increase to a level of amazement for us. I want you to also pray this prayer:

Jesus, Proverbs 1:7 says, "The fear of the Lord is the beginning of knowledge; fools despise wisdom and instruction." Lord I do not want to be a fool. Please give me the knowledge and understanding to continue to let you guide my steps for success. In Jesus Name, Amen.

INCREASE MY WISDOM

IN ORDER FOR us to gain wisdom, we have to go through some challenges in our life. The definition of wisdom is the quality of having experience, knowledge, and good judgment. Wisdom is something that God wants to give us and all we need to do is simply ask. Solomon asks God for wisdom, and God granted it. I am going to include what Solomon said to God, and what God spoke back to him, because of its relevance. 1 Kings 3:7-14 says, "Now, Lord my God, you have made your servant king in place of my father David. But I am only a little child and do not know how to carry out my duties. Your servant is here among the people you have chosen, a great people, too numerous to count or number. So give your servant a discerning heart to govern your people and to distinguish between right and wrong. For who is able to govern this great people of yours?" The Lord was pleased that Solomon had asked for this." So God said to him, "Since you have asked for this and **not for long life or wealth for yourself, nor have asked for the death of your enemies but for discernment in administering justice,** I will do what you have asked. I will give you a wise and discerning heart, so that there will never have been anyone like you, nor will there ever be. Moreover, I will give you what you have not asked for-both wealth and honor- so that in your lifetime you will have no equal among kings. **And if you walk in obedience to me and keep my decrees and commands as David your father did, I will give you a long life.**"

These scriptures are so powerful and extremely relevant today. Solomon could have asked for anything, but he chose to ask for wisdom. He was a young boy, and understood that in order for him to rule the people he needed wisdom. Let me let you in on a secret; God is not going to give you something great that you can do on your own. God will always make sure that you cannot do it without him. The Lord wants all the honor and glory. Besides, if we could do everything ourselves, why would we need God? Keep this with you in your heart, and realize that you need to keep God in everything.

So let us break down the areas that I have put in bold. Since Solomon did not ask for wealth and long life or even the death of his enemies, God granted him his request. We often come to God and ask him for more money and riches, but what are we asking to advance the kingdom of God? Sure, more wealth can be granted, but we need to have a desire to do God's will instead of saying, "LOOK AT ME." Our attention should always be on what we can do for God, and that request will be answered. God still granted Solomon wealth and long life because that was not his focus, but God knows the desires of our heart and he will grant above and beyond what we ask for. Which brings me to the next point in bold. God told Solomon that if he was obedient and kept the commands and decrees that he would give Solomon long life. This is the key my friend. We have to want to be obedient to God. We are not going to go through life never sinning again. We all fall short of the glory of God. However, we should be trying everyday with all of our hearts to please God in everything that we do. We should not be practicing sin, and expect God to bless us with his best.

We must understand that all of our intelligence that we think we have created comes from our Lord and Savior Jesus Christ. 1 Corinthians 1:19 "For it is written, I will destroy the wisdom of the wise; the intelligence of the intelligent I will frustrate." We have to recognize that God does not think like we do as mortal men and women. God is the only one who can give us eternal wisdom. We can go to all the colleges and universities that we want to, but without God being first priority, that wisdom will not be as sharp as it can be with God. 1 Corinthians 3:19 states, "For the wisdom of this world is foolishness in God's sight. As it is written: "he catches the wise in their craftiness." The key is to have a daily relationship with God to gain the wisdom and knowledge that no one else can offer you.

We will increase our wisdom once we comprehend that our experiences make us wiser. Let us go back to being a child. When our parents told us do not touch the stove, what did we do? We touched it anyway. Once we touched it and realized it was hot, we immediately pulled away from it. The next time we came across the stove our minds went back to the previous experience and we learned from that mistake. Our mistakes make us improve as a person. Do not be scared to take risks and commit faults. When we create errors, we learn quicker and more everlastingly. Eventually, when you come across the same circumstances again in the future, you will recognize it and be better.

In order for us to increase wisdom, we also have to know ourselves. James 1:5 states, "If any of you lacks wisdom, you should ask God, who gives generously to all without finding fault, and it will be given to you." In order to make good decisions concerning your life, it is of the highest significance to first know yourself. Come to God and ask him to help you find out who you are. What inspires you? What makes you happy inside? What makes you sad? What things will help or harm you? What is most important to you? These are a few of the things that you need to recognize before you can create wise decisions. To achieve this you need to pray to God everyday and ask him for more wisdom so that you can improve on your day to day decision making. Find a quiet place at home, and meditate on these feelings. Only in silence and calmness can you contemplate on yourself and life. Contemplation is one of the best ways to get to know you and become wiser than before.

We also have to be willing to learn new things in order for us to become wiser. Why do you think we are required in high school to take Algebra and some of the advanced math? I use to always say, all I need to know is basic addition, multiplication and subtraction so I can count money. Of course, we do need those things. However, I realize now that learning something original will widen your intellectual muscles and allow you to make better decisions every day. So go out every day and try to find something new you can learn. We have to challenge the way we think. Crossword puzzles and plenty of brain games are a way to increase wisdom because it forces the brain to work out!!! Outside of games, you can apply this to everyday circumstances like a different route home instead of the usual route that you know or preparing a meal that you have never cooked before. We should test what is common to us in how we think.

Another way to increase your wisdom is taking on challenges that are hard. I remember when I use to go on vacation in the early 1990's; I had to get an atlas. I had to map out my route, and look for specific landmarks to guide me along the way. Today, I am confident to go into any locations because I have a GPS on my phone, and in my car. That is the only reason I can move to any city and believe I can get around with no problem. I am lost without it. However, challenging my wisdom is trying to get to a location that I have been to only once before without using my GPS this time around. I have done it from time to time, and it does make me think more. Since I had the experience of being there before, my wisdom will let me know if I make a wrong turn because my surroundings will look unfamiliar. I guess the same can be said about using search engines. I will use Bing and Google even when my wife asks me the simplest questions!! The next time you want to investigate something, don't look it up on the internet. Challenge yourself so your mind will be obligated to think artistically.

Once you do gain wisdom, make sure that you protect it. Ecclesiastes 7:12 says, "For the protection of wisdom is like the protection of money, and the advantage of knowledge is that wisdom preserves the life of him who has it." Protect and preserve the wisdom you do have by disseminating the skills, experience, knowledge, practices and other intellectual resources being held in your brain and the brains of other righteous men and women. We do a disservice to ourselves if we make money, but do not teach someone close to us how to also become wealthy. It is the same with the wisdom we have gained through our Lord and Savior Jesus Christ. It does us no good to hold onto the wisdom that we have gained from reading the word, and gaining wisdom through our testimonies of our lives, and the lives of the people we come in contact with.

So how do we increase our wisdom? There are many ways to increase your wisdom. You can learn new things. You can meditate and find quiet time to become wiser than before. We can also try to do things differently in our thinking with crossword puzzles and other brain games. We can make ourselves take the tough route of doing things. Instead of using the GPS to get to a location, use your brain knowledge to attempt to get to your destination.

However, your increase of wisdom should start and end with God. Psalm 111:10 says, "The fear of the Lord is the beginning of wisdom; all who follow his precepts have a good understanding. To him belongs eternal praise." Let us not forget what King Solomon did. He asked for wisdom, and God blessed him with the wealth and long life. I want you to also pray this prayer:

Jesus, Proverbs 2:10 says, "For wisdom will come into your heart, and knowledge will be pleasant to your soul." Lord, give me the wisdom to learn from my experiences and apply good principles to practice today and in the future. I am nothing without you. Please breathe in my direction and give me discernment to make sound and timely decisions. In Jesus Name, Amen.

Put down your own way of doing things, and recognize that everything that you do that brings an increase in wisdom comes from our Lord and Savior Jesus Christ. Since he sacrificed his life for us by dying on the cross for our sins, we have the opportunity to come boldly to the throne and ask God for more wisdom so we can do more for the Kingdom of God.

INCREASE MY STRENGTH

THE DEFINITION OF strength is the quality or state of being strong. My bother in law annually competes in a 1000 pound club at Fort Carson, Colorado where he has to lift over 1000 pounds through three different events such as the bench press, squats, and dead lift. Since he is a Marine, I know that he can handle it!!! God bless you my brother and I hope you exceed your goal this year. We feel the weight of the world on our lives sometimes when we are trying to handle all the different challenges in life alone. This is when we need to turn it over to Jesus, and let the Holy Spirit work in us.

When we measure strength in this world, it is measured by so many different things. Many nations measure their strength by their Army or military power. The world looks at who has the most missiles, guns, aircraft etc... When strength is measured in money, it is used in influencing financial decisions in businesses and buying out other smaller companies with less resources and power. Finally, we know that people use sexual power to take advantage of young people with money through pornography. In every case those who embrace the worldly muscle hold on to their power by threatening, dominating and seducing those with modest strength. The physically powerful in this world is puffed up by breaking those under them down. But the Glory of God is seen by giving superiority to the weak.

Philippians 4:13 says, "I can do all things through Christ Jesus which strengthens me." God is for the underdog. The people that society has a tendency to put down, God is cheering them on. He wants to exalt you above your own expectations, but you have to trust and believe in him. There are many examples of God using ordinary people, and taking them to a level of supremacy. One of my favorite stories and inspirational stories in the Bible of the least to the greatest is the story of David.

Samuel was sent to anoint the next king of Israel. 1 Samuel 16: 6-8 says, "When they arrived, Samuel saw Eliab and thought, "Surely the Lord's anointed stands here before the Lord." But the Lord said to Samuel, "**Do not consider his appearance or his height, for I have rejected him. The Lord does not look at the things people look at. People look at the outward appearance, but the Lord looks at the heart.**" I will not put verses 9-13 in here, but it goes on to tell how David's father Jesse had seven of his sons pass before Samuel, and Samuel told him that the Lord had not chosen any of them. Samuel asks Jesse did he have any more sons. Jesse said my youngest son David is tending to the sheep in the Sheppard's field. Samuel sent for him, and David was the one. David was not the biggest and did not have more training than his brothers, but the Lord knew that David had a heart after God's own heart. We know the rest of the story about how David defeated Goliath, but the point to hammer across is the Lord does not look at the outside; he looks at your heart. We are a society that is so driven by what a person looks like. When you turn to God, we need to depend on our strength to come from him, and him alone. When we become obedient and seek God's wise counsel, he will make us strong and powerful in everything that we do.

We have to realize that our bodies can become fatigue and weak, but our soul is strong in Christ Jesus. Sometimes our soul can become weary. So how can we get strong? We can get strong through reading the word of God and applying it to our life. Psalm 119:28 states, "My soul is weary with sorrow, strengthen me according to your word." The word of God is our strength, and we need to be in the word daily. It is also good to get bible verses memorized also. Why? Not to impress people. However, it is good to have some scriptures memorized because when trouble comes you will have some weapons to fight off the enemy. The scriptures will make you stronger than you could ever imagine. We memorize our favorite songs, and favorite lines from movies, and many other worldly things. However, none of those things can help us when we are facing trouble. I challenge you today to try and memorize at least one meaningful verse in the Bible, and apply it to your life. It will make a difference in your life drastically.

Having a spirit of hope that things will get better in life is something that we need to always have. It does not matter how bad your situation is, at all times have a desire for things to improve. Isaiah 40:29-31 says, "He gives strength to the weary and increases the power of the weak. Even youths grow tired and weary, and young men fall and stumble; but those who hope in the Lord will renew their strength. They will soar on wings like eagles; they will run and not grow weary, they will walk and not be faint." When we put our faith and trust in God, he will empower us. He will bring you from the bottom of your organization to the top when you have hope and know he is directing your path. The key to this is to not grow weary when it is not happening on your time schedule. Wait on the Lord because he will make it happen at the right time. Sometimes we believe we are ready to step into a position of power, but God knows when we are ready. We need to keep our eyes and faith in the Lord, and he will deliver.

Another factor to increasing your strength is having joy in everything that you do. Nehemiah 8:10 states, "Go and enjoy choice food and sweet drinks, and send some to those who have nothing prepared. This day is holy to our Lord. Do not grieve, for the joy of the Lord is your strength." I know that sometimes it may be hard to stay upbeat and happy, but remember that nothing can steal your joy. Joy is something that you have, and you have to give it away. No one can take your joy from you. I've been told before, that you cannot control someone's actions; you can only control your reaction. Wake up daily with a great attitude, and convince yourself that no matter what happens I am not going to let anyone steal my joy. We have to make a conscience effort in our mind, heart, and spirit that our attitude towards everything that we do will keep us joyful.

Remember when I expressed earlier in another chapter to seek first the kingdom of God and righteousness and all the other things will be taken care of? It is the same with strength. Mark 12:30 says, "Love the Lord your God with all your heart and with all your soul and with all your mind and with all your strength." God wants us to put everything aside that we love to do, people that we love, and things that we cherish, to put him first in our day to day busy lives. He did not say love him between the hours of 12 a.m. and 8 a.m. or when it is convenient. He said to love him with everything that we have. We should not love anyone before him. Not even our spouse, children, or parents. Yes, I said it. In a marriage it should be a partnership of three. Men, you are not the head of your household. If you want it to be successful, God needs to be the head of your house. When men truly put God first, your relationship flows smoother than if you try and do it on your own. I am not licensed to be a marriage counselor, but I have tried to run a marriage without Jesus and it just does not work. The commitment has to be to God first so the hurtful and disrespectful things that can happen in a marriage will not happen. I am not saying that everything will be peaches and cream, but the resolution to your problems will end in harmony and peace. It is through his strength that your marriage will be strong and grow. Give your marriage to God. You won't be disappointed.

So how do we increase our strength? We increase our strength when we stop trying to depend on our own natural strength, and give it to the Lord for supernatural strength. The flesh will always become weak because of our sinful nature. There are many distractions in this world to keep our minds off of the goodness that the Lord has for us. When we put our trust and strength into human hands of this world that control politics, the military, financial wealth, and all the other possessions that can be controlled, you will be let down every time. Remember, that God controls everything. Even those human possessions can be turned around for your good. I want you to also pray this prayer:

Jesus, Philippians 4:13 says, "I can do all things through Christ Jesus who strengthens me." I demand that you make my soul strong when my flesh is weak. Keep me in my Bible where I can get stronger by being fed the word of God daily. In Jesus Name, Amen.

The strength that you want from the Lord comes from developing a daily relationship with him. Ask him daily for an increase in strength, and watch God take you to a level that you never could have reached on your own.

INCREASE MY VISION

No, I AM not talking about your 20/20 eye vision, but I hope that your vision improves daily! The definition of vision is an experience of seeing someone or something in a dream or trance, or as a supernatural spirit. The increase in vision that I am talking about is being able to see something in your future. Proverbs 29:18 says, "Where there is no vision, the people perish: but he that keepeth the law, happy is he." We have to have something to look forward to. This vision should be the thing that drives our motivation and determination. Look at your vision as a goal that you are moving towards. Sometime our vision in this world could be the direction you want your business to go. Maybe it could be the direction you want the big corporation that you are CEO of to move forward and prosper. Your vision should change the way you think and live. A single man's vision should change once he decides to settle down and have a family. A vision keeps us going when there is no apparent reason to keep pushing further in the direction of the goal.

We have to have a vision in good times and hard times. Hebrews 12:2 states, "Jesus endured the cross because of his vision- "the joy set before him." We can all relate to tough times at one time or another. It does not always have to be financial. We all know that we can also go through tough emotional times. When everything around us is spiraling down, it is our vision for God that keeps us going. We have to ask God to give us the vision that is his will. What we normally try to do is take care of everything ourselves with our own vision. This disables what God wants for us in our lives. Give it to God, and watch the wonderful things that he will do in your life.

In all things that you go through in this life, you have to have a vision that you will live through and get through it. Psalm 27:13 says, "I remain confident of this: I will see the goodness of the Lord in the land of the living." With the proper vision God will get us through anything. It is only when we get down on ourselves that it blocks what God's vision is for us. I cannot express enough in this chapter that attitude makes a huge difference. I have to reiterate that God will not perform the miracles that you want if you are steady complaining and murmuring about what you do not have. We have to see the goal and vision and move towards it with consistency.

So, how do you increase your vision? It is simple. First, you have to get your mind and heart aligned with God. Second, you have to be able to see and believe that what God's will is for you is going to come to pass. Third, you need to keep a great attitude while you are moving towards that goal. It is so important to not get discouraged and down when things do not go your way. Create a vision board that you can look at daily, and move towards those goals. I want you to also pray this prayer:

Jesus, Proverbs 29:18 states, "Where there is no vision, the people perish: but he that keepeth the law, happy is he." Lord I want to be happy. Help me to have a clear vision of what you want me to do. I want to be a vessel so you can use me as a servant to advance the kingdom. Guide me and show me the way. In Jesus Name, Amen.

We need to keep God first priority in our daily lives, and know that God will gives us the vision that he wants us to have as long as we stay in a relationship with him. Do not get discouraged, but stay encouraged; for God is with you.

INCREASE MY HEALTH

THE DEFINITION OF health is the state of being free from illness or injury. Having a healthy lifestyle can come in many different forms. Some of us go to the gym, and work out on a daily basis. Some of us go get massages from a massage therapist. And then there are those that stick to healthy eating habits without breaking the routine for months and sometimes years. Healthy living has to become a passion of yours. However, we have to remember that no matter what we are doing that we cannot put more emphasis on anything before God.

Romans 12:2 states, "Do not conformed to this world, but be transformed by the renewal of your mind, that by testing you may discern what is the will of God, what is good and acceptable and perfect." God wants us to transform our minds, and realize that every function that you do in life will not be complete unless he is the first priority in your daily passion. As you grow in Christ Jesus, you will be able to discern between a test, and God's perfect will.

Another area that people do not like to talk about is their mental health. Our emotions play a big part in how healthy our bodies are. Several people suffer from many types of emotional disorders. There are plenty of different medicines and prescriptions prescribed by doctors to help heal us of our anxiety and pain that we may have emotionally. However, the best medicine that is 100 percent guaranteed to cure you, is the healing power of Jesus Christ. He is the answer to all of our emotional and physical problems. We have a tendency to put our trust in medicine, and start to depend on it to make us well. When we do that we are putting our faith and believe in the world system more than we are trusting God. We should put our trust in the Lord first, and he will give us discernment and strength to move forward in our physical and emotional challenges. I have had plenty of physical ailments in my life. 95% of the injuries I have had, came from playing sports! I know that is probably normal for many people. However, there are some of us that get sick and injured in other ways. To this point in my life, I have not suffered from any emotional disorders or depression. I found salvation on my 14th birthday, and ever since that day I knew that Jesus was walking with me. I found that if you always have a positive outlook and do not let things worry you, life has a tendency to produce positive results.

There are quite a few things that I have learned that will increase your health physically and spiritually. The first thing I want to talk about is learning how to forgive. This can be one of the key elements to increasing our health significantly. Matthew 6:14-15 says, "For if you forgive men when they sin against you, your heavenly Father will also forgive you. But if you do not forgive men their sins, your father will not forgive your sins." Listen, we have to get over it and learn how to deal with whatever someone has done to us or against us. That is the only way we will heal. We are sitting around depressed and upset about what this person has done to us, but they are living their lives not thinking about us. We have to learn how to forgive so we can not only excuse that person for what they did to us, but also to release the weight or burden that we are carrying around from that person. I promise you will feel better. Do not go around holding on to sexual or physical abuse of the past. Turn to Jesus to help you rise above the pain. Jesus may direct you to some physical counseling such as a psychiatrist. However, I will tell you the best solution to help with the tragedy and pain. Pray and demand that any unclean spirits that are trying to reside in your body or latch on to your body be washed clean in the name of Jesus. Keep praying this prayer daily or as often as you need to transform your mind, and help you move forward. Forgive your parents. Some of us may have not had both parents to raise us, but we have to let it go. We can only improve, and make sure we are an active figure in our children's lives. Do not keep repeating the cycle. Forgive them and make things better for the future. Anyone that has done wrong to you, forgive them so you can heal and get on to a more prosperous life.

Another way to increase our health is to learn how to pray and spend some quiet time with God. Life can become so busy at times, and there are so many distractions out there trying to get you to lose your focus with God. My wife and I came home just the other day, and the first thing I did was turn the television on. She said to me at the moment, "I realize that you like noise." I actually do not like a lot of noise. However, when it comes to sports, I do like the television turned up louder than usual to get the full effect. I realize that it can be irritating to someone else so I try to be more considerate. We should be more considerate towards God by spending quality time with him. What I had to do myself, is to find a room in the house where it could just be God and I. What I decided to do was to get up 30 minutes earlier during the work week to spend time praying and reading my Bible before I start my day. I tell God how awesome he is and I praise him. I have found that my day is going much smoother than it did in the past. My stress level has gone down, and I give all the glory to God for guiding my path. This works for me, but it may not work for you. Finding quiet time for you is important. You may need to keep the radio off in the car while you are driving or instead of taking a nap when you get home open your Bible and tell God how much you love him and glorify his name! Start to do this on a regular basis, and you will get confirmation on things you need answers to. You will hear that still soft voice speaking to you and that peace that you will experience will help increase your health.

Have you ever been around someone that was so negative and judgmental? This can create an unhealthy environment. Leave all judgment to God. Matthew 7:1 states, "Do not judge, or you too will be judged." We have been around critical people that are fault-finding every little thing about their colleagues, family, bosses, etc. In order for our health to flourish, we do not need to be judgmental of anyone. We need to tell the people that are around us that are judgmental that we are not going to waste our time being critical of someone else's flaws. We all have flaws, and no one can be fixed without the grace and mercy of our Lord and Savior Jesus Christ.

We need to allow the joy that is in us to come out and be on display daily to increase our health. Psalm 100:1 says, "Make a joyful noise unto the Lord, all ye lands." God wants us to have joy all the time. Do not let anyone steal your joy. I want you to know that no one can take your joy; you have to give it away. When you are in traffic, and someone cuts you off, say praise the Lord instead of some of the other choice words you think of. When your supervisor says that you are going to have mandatory overtime tonight, do not get upset just look at the positive and you will not lose your joy. There will always be distractions in your path to upset you. Transform your thinking to help you turn every negative into a positive, and it will help improve your health. I say the Jabez Prayer daily to help me keep my joy.

1 Chronicles 4:10 says,

"And Jabez called on the God of Israel saying, Oh that you would bless me indeed, and enlarge my territory, that your hand would be with me, and that you would keep me from evil, That I may not cause pain!" So God granted him what he requested."

I have learned that by praying this prayer daily, God keeps evil away from me. That is definitely keeping me healthy by keeping evil spirits from trying to harm me. Try it and trust me, it works!

Something that is also an answer to increasing your health I want to tell you is to have an open mind to what God can do for you. Permit yourself to accept as true, things that aren't simply understandable. When things happen that you cannot explain, that is nothing but God. We have to identify that, and give God all the glory and praise behind it.

The last thing that I want to talk to you about in increasing your health is for you to turn to God when you have pain and sadness. These are the times when we feel down, and we can hurt our health physically and emotionally. When you lose a love one or a tragedy of some type happens in our life, some of us slip into a state of depression. One of my brothers was murdered in October of 2000. My brothers Derrick and Earl were very close because they were only a year apart. I was 7 years older than my middle brother Earl, and eight years older than my baby brother Derrick. That was such a sad time for my family. That was the first time in my life that someone close to me had ever passed away. I turned to God to help me through this difficult time, and he did. I thought about the good times that we shared together to get me through it. However, my brother Derrick did not take it well at all.

My brother Derrick saw my brother Earl lying out on the ground after he was shot. He slipped into a state of depression, and was later diagnosed with being bipolar. We talked about putting God first, and I tried to help him the best I could. He had some other issues weighing him down, and he took his own life in June 2004. Ladies and gentlemen, I have experienced firsthand why you have to stay in daily contact with the Lord to help you through painful and difficult times. You cannot do it without the love of Jesus Christ. 1 Corinthians 13:13 says, "And now these three remain: faith, hope and love. But the greatest of these is love." It will take all three to get through mournful times. Keeping God first priority in these situations will allow you to get stronger as the days go on.

One more point I would like to make about spiritual and physical health is do not sweat the small stuff. Let go of jealousy. Do not be envious of someone else's success. Recognize that God can do the same for you once we commit to being obedient. Let go of anger. This was something I had to let go of myself. I had to ask God to deliver me from it. It was holding me back. I gave it to God, and when I am weak he is strong. I trust in Jesus to take on that unclean spirit. Do not be a gossiper or listen to people constantly stirring up drama. Do not find a reason to get frustrated over things that are not worth your time. That is nothing but the adversary trying to distract your mind so you will not worship Jesus.

So how do you increase your health? Increase your health by learning to forgive like God has forgiven us. Make time for God. Find a quiet place somewhere in your home to pray and meditate with God. Seeking God has to become a lifestyle. Make seeking him your first passion. Stay keeping your joy on display everyday! Keep an open mind about things that you know can only be short of a miracle to happen to you from God. We need to have fun while being a Christian and that will also increase your health. Some people believe that when you become a Christian, that all fun stops. That is not true. I have found that I live a healthier lifestyle since I have rededicated my life to the Lord. I have hope of things to come because I walk by faith and not by sight. It is a refreshing peace of mind to know that the ruler of the universe is on my side in whatever I am going through. The scripture says no weapon formed against me will prosper. That is in my health and everything else that I do. I want you to also pray this prayer:

Lord Jesus, John 6:35 says, Jesus said to them, "I am the bread of life; whoever comes to me shall not hunger, and whoever believes in me shall never thirst." Lord, keep me spiritually, emotionally, and physically healthy. Keep my mind and soul on you first daily and allow me to get fed your daily word. In Jesus Name, Amen.

I am not distracted by health issues that may come up now because I have learned to let the Lord deal with it. When we abide in him and trust him for all things, we will experience the best that God has for us. Keep God first priority in your life and watch him do amazing things beyond your imagination.

INCREASE MY PATIENCE

THE DEFINITION OF patience is the capacity to accept or tolerate delay, trouble, or suffering without getting angry or upset. Besides faith, this is probably the most challenging of all the principles for us to discipline ourselves to triumph over. We live in a world today that we are use to having things happen quickly. We have fast food restaurants, computers, the internet, etc. Most of us cannot even stand in line at a fast food restaurant without getting upset because the line is not moving fast enough. The microwave fast living style has spoiled us and we do not want to wait on anything. God wants us to be patient and understand that he is not on our time table. We are all on God's time table. Romans 12:12 states, "Rejoice in hope, be patient in tribulation, be constant in prayer." When we ask for things from God, we need to be persistent, and keep our enthusiasm and spirit excited for the breakthrough. However, what happens is that we become discouraged because it does not seem like things are happening fast enough. When we are going through tough times, God can be testing us to see if we are going to continuing to show patience and wait on him, or if we are going to give up on our hope for something better and take things into our own hands. We need to constantly stay in prayer doing this time of hope. So why do we believe that God is not answering our prayers? Maybe it is because we are not praying correctly.

There are a few things that we need to do to make sure that our prayers are answered. First, we need to make sure that we have the word of God in us. When we pray, we need to back up those prayers with the Bible scriptures. Every tribulation that we go through, a solution to the problem is in the Word of God. We need to get in there and read so we can get an answer to what God wants us to do. Once we do that we need to give God our undivided attention and pray. Second, in order for our prayers to be valid, we need to make sure we pray in the name of Jesus. The prayers are not even guaranteed unless we pray in the name of Jesus. Finally, we have to trust in the Holy Spirit to deliver. The Holy Spirit is the one that is going to certify that the job gets done.

When you were a baby, you were not expected to get a job right? When it comes to patience, we have to expect that things will happen gradually. A toddler cannot go from being a young boy to a grown man in a year. We have to expect God to work on us over a period of time. 1 Corinthians 13:11 says, "When I was a child, I talked like a child; I thought like a child, I reasoned like a child. When I became a man, I put the ways of childhood behind me." Having patience is a process that with maturity in Christ, you will get there. It is not going to happen overnight. We have to realize that God is for us. He never wants us to fail. God is not saying I am just going to make them wait because I am out shopping for new saints so I will get back to them. He is not on vacation, and figures he will get back to you when he gets back in town!! God wants us to win in every situation. However, some of the stuff we are asking for we are not ready to receive. It will happen as long as you have faith, and continue to put the Kingdom first. God usually is waiting until you are ready.

We need to have hope in what God will do for us. Romans 8:25 says, "But if we hope for what we do not see, we wait for it with patience." God knows your present and your future. He knows where you are going. We display hope and belief when we accept Jesus as our personal Savior. We did not see Jesus with our own physical eyes. There is no one alive today that walked on the earth when Jesus was alive and performing miraculous acts. Yet, the power of the Holy Spirit and the promise to have eternal life is when we put our hope in things eternal. When we stay patient, we are telling God that we trust in his Holy word, and that we are moving through this world with full confidence that he will deliver on his promises.

I do believe that everyone wakes up every morning wanting to do their best and be positive. What happens to us is when things do not happen fast, we have a tendency to give up. Galatians 6:9 states, "And let us not grow weary of doing good, for in due season we will reap, if we do not give up." Get up every day wanting to do good for someone. It may be as simple as giving someone the greeting of the day (a simple hello will do). Keep on being adamant through everything. Whatever that dream or goal is that you have, do not let it go. There are many stories in the bible about people that were sick or had some kind of disease. The one that sticks out to me is the woman who was bleeding. Matthew 9:20 says, "Just then a woman who had been subject to bleeding for **twelve years** came up behind him and touched the edge of his cloak. She said to herself, "If I only touch his cloak, I will be healed." Of course this is a story of faith. However, it is also a story of hope. She had been dealing with this bleeding for twelve years. She did not throw in the towel and say well this is the hand I was dealt in life so I guess I just have to go with it!! She had hope that things would get better and she endured many tough years. She did not give up. God made sure that we could read about people that had been through things for many years. He wanted us to see that if you just be patient that the blessings and miracles will come. Do not give up on your dreams. Do not give up on your passion. Most of all, do not give up on God!

Sometimes we see people around us succeeding, and some of them are not even following the word of God. You believe that you are giving God your best. Meanwhile, your neighbor does not even know how to spell church let alone attend on a consistent basis. The bible speaks about having patience in times like this. Psalm 37:7 says, "Be still before the Lord and wait patiently for him; do not fret when people succeed in their ways, when they carry out their wicked schemes." Do not be upset about this at all. God has your back. Yes, it may seem that your neighbor is doing better, but like we talked about previously, we should never grow weary of doing good. Some of the good you can do instead of getting frustrated with your neighbor's success is to tell them about Jesus and tell them about the Gospel. That is doing something good for someone else and it will come back to you. When we start to get inpatient, we may conform to this world and look for pleasures that are not good for us to satisfy our need to succeed. God wants us to sit and be patient. Wait on him. He is supplying all of our needs. That is one of the promises God has made us. He did not say he would give us all of our wants. There are plenty of things that we ask for that are selfish pleasures, and they do not have anything to do with advancing the Kingdom of God. James 4:3 says, "When you ask, you do not receive, because you ask with wrong motives, that you may spend what you get on your pleasures." Put everything into perspective for the Kingdom of God. Work hard to do kingdom business, and those desires of your heart can be met. Our hearts have to first be on serving God and lifting him up not ourselves. Romans 8:7 says, "Because the carnal mind is enmity against God: for it is not subject to the law of God, neither indeed can be." Carnal mind is worldly. We have to get rid of our carnal mind and transform to the spiritual mind to come into the fullness of God.

When we are patient with God, we can recognize that his plan for our life is better than ours. Jeremiah 29:11 states, "For I know the plans I have for you, declares the Lord, plans for welfare and not for evil, to give you a future and a hope." We have to stop getting caught up with what our plans are, and trust in the Lord for his plan. Realize that God is out in front of us always encouraging us. He does not want to see us stumble, but when we do he is there to pick us up. With patience God's plan will begin to unfold in front of our eyes. Do not worry and stay focused on him. The evil that we seem to find from time to time is because we have a tendency to get ahead of God. I have found that when we get ahead of God, we are headed for disaster. It can be so much confusion and distractions when the Lord is not guiding us to his perfect plan. Sometimes that plan that God has is fulfilled, but we do not always recognize it because we are focus on something else. We miss it, and we wonder what is taking God so long to deliver. Take time and sit back and reflect on what has happened, and where you are trying to go. When you are not complaining about your condition and you are just being patient, God will graduate you to the next step. God will also move when you show patience and faith in him, and you initiate steps toward your goal. Remember, faith without works is dead.

Have you ever been in a situation that you wanted something so bad that you could not sit still? That has happened to all of us, but that is not how God wants us to be. Philippians 4:6 says, "Do not be anxious about anything, but in everything by prayer and supplication with thanksgiving let your requests be made known to God." Yes, go ahead and ask God for what you want. However, do not let the want of it occupy your mind and spirit so much that it becomes your God. Continue to pray for it, and allow God to give it to you in due season. Let go and let God! I remember when I was in the Army, and I was trying to make the rank of Sergeant First Class. I was looking over my evaluations everyday to convince myself that it was good enough to get promoted. When the promotion list came out the first year I was eligible to get promoted, I did not make it. I was a little discouraged, but I understood that life goes on. I prayed about it, and left it in God's hands. The next year I did not concern myself with it, and I received a call one evening to let me know I had to see the senior enlisted advisor called the Command Sergeant Major the next morning. I thought I was in some kind of trouble. When he brought me in with three other individuals, he said, "Congratulations! You have made the list for promotion." I learned at that moment that when you do not make other things a priority before God, he will grant you the desires of your heart. He has to get all of the glory, not you. All promotions come from God. Just wait on him, and he will deliver on it when you are ready to receive it.

I want to talk to you about an issue that can be a little uncomfortable to talk about. That topic is anger. I know you are saying what does this have to do with patience? Ecclesiastes 7:9 says, "Be not quick in your spirit to become angry, for anger lodges in the bosom of fools." Everyone gets angry at some time or another in life. We are human. However we should not get fired up at every little thing that happens to us. Do you know someone like that? They have road rage when they are driving. They want to argue with the server when they are ordering food. If their children say something inappropriate they become enraged. This is where it can get dark. We have seen many domestic violence and child abuse cases involving an individual not being able to control their temper. Acknowledging that you have a problem is important. What is just as important is that you ask God to cleanse you of this unclean spirit, and tell God to make you aware when you are getting upset so he can calm you. Being patient at this critical time is also significant. If it is something that I know I can resolve quickly, I give that problem a number 1. If it is something that if I stay in the environment may get me to an upset nature, I give it an 8 or above. This is when I know to have patience and walk away.

When you represent the Lord Jesus Christ, you must learn how to become calm and have a cool head. 2 Timothy 2:24 states, "And the Lord's servant must not be quarrelsome but kind to everyone, able to teach, patiently enduring evil. This is not easy, but when you truly love the Lord, you will try to become your best in this area. We will run into difficult people. People that have personalities that are so different from yours, that you may not want to stay in the same room with them. Would God want us to reject them? Of course he would not want that. We have to learn how to speak to the individual that walks past us without speaking. We have to learn how to be calm when the situation shows you in the natural that this could get ugly. This happened to me recently. I was in Walgreens with my wife one Sunday afternoon, and I was glancing at the magazines along the check out line. Suddenly, out of nowhere, the young man behind me yelled out, "Why do you keep turning around looking at me?" At first, I did not know who he was talking to. I asked him, "Are you talking to me?" He said, "Yeah, I am talking to you!" I did not even see this couple behind me at first. My flesh initially wanted to say to him, you must be insecure because I was not even thinking about you. However, my wife told me, do not respond to ignorance. She left and went to the car, while I paid for my items. When I was about to leave the Holy Spirit was telling me to say something positive. I told him God bless you brother. When I got to the car, I said to my wife, what was that about? She said that was nothing but the devil trying to attack you. Something big is coming. The next day, the principal from my old job contacted me to offer me my old JROTC Instructor position back!!! Had I been inpatient and quarrelsome with that young man, it would have stolen my joy and possibly ruined my opportunity for a new position if that situation escalated to law enforcement being called. That is why we need to be patient because only God knows what is in our future. He is trying to see if we will pass the test.

From the beginning God has wanted us to wait patiently on him. Hebrews 6:13-15 states, "When God made his promise to Abraham, since there was no one greater for him to swear by, he swore by himself, saying, "I will surely bless you and give you many descendants. And so after waiting patiently, Abraham received what was promised." Notice that God first made the promise, and Abraham waited patiently because he believed that God would deliver on his promise. Abraham is the father of all nations because he was faithful, and he trusted God to do something special for him.

So how do you increase your patience? There are many things that I have said in this chapter about patience. The bottom line is to believe and trust that God will do what he said he will do. Do not get ahead of him, and let go of yourself and let God do his supernatural for you. I want you to also pray this prayer:

Lord, Galatians 5:22-23 says, "But the fruit of the Spirit is love, joy, peace, forbearance, kindness, goodness, faithfulness, gentleness and self-control." Jesus, give me more patience and calm me when situations arise that prompt me to make a decision without thinking it through fully. Work on me Lord, and keep me calm. Allow me to find something good in every situation to help me control my dissatisfactions. In Jesus Name, Amen.

Having patience will allow you to grow spiritually and physically so that you can live your best life!

INCREASE MY EXPECTANCY

LET US FIRST define what expectancy is. Expectancy is the state of thinking or hoping that something, especially something pleasant, will happen or be the case. We should live everyday expecting something great to happen to us today. Do not live your day expecting the worse or expecting just to get by. What kind of hope is that? When I transformed my thinking, I started looking for something special to happen to me daily. It may be a unique conversation that I have with someone or something as simple as "I love you" from my family. I am expecting only good things to happen to me daily, and even when difficulties come up, I stay positive in everything that I go through.

God is the author of your life. He knows how the story begins and how the story ends. Jeremiah 29:11 says, " For I know the plans I have for you, declares the Lord, plans for welfare and not for evil, to give you a future and a hope." God wants you to hope for the best and know that no matter what you are going through that he is still on the throne and in control.

You may be saying Anthony, I have been expecting good things to happen to me for years, but nothing exciting has happened to me. Raise your level of thinking, and ask yourself do I have the Holy Spirit living inside of me? Acts 2:38 says, "And Peter said to them, "Repent and be baptized every one of you in the name of Jesus Christ for the forgiveness of your sins, and you will receive the gift of the Holy Spirit." When you have the Holy Spirit living inside of you, and you are trying to be your best for God, you will start to see results. Everyone's story and results are different so I can only tell you my story. Part of my daily prayer life has, "I am expecting something great today!" While I sit here writing this chapter in the book, I can tell you a special journey about expectancy. I had been saying this prayer of increase on the back of this book for several years, and I was in church in September of 2010. I was visiting a small church in Cordele, GA where my wife was a member of at one time. The Pastor's message that particular Sunday was use what you have. His message talked about the many things that we have down inside of us that we do not tap into because we do not know how special the Holy Spirit is residing in us. Something down inside of me shook at that moment. I thought what do I have that is special and unique in my life besides my family? Well, I thought about how special the prayer is! Over the next few months, I researched what I had to do to get the prayer copyrighted. In November of 2010, I received paperwork back telling me that the prayer is classified as a poem in the Library of Congress. I was so excited, and my level of expectancy had risen to a new level. I wrote letters to several different Pastors and Public figures asking them to help me get this prayer out. My goal is to get the prayer out around the world so people can apply it to their daily life, and it could be a blessing to someone else. There was only one person that responded to my letters and she is a famous worldwide Pastor. The letter basically said the prayer was beautiful, but because of different laws and guidelines she could not refer me to anyone. However, I was thankful that her ministry took the time and wrote me back. I did not lose my fire. I started passing the prayer out locally to many people. Anyone who wanted a copy, I gave it to them. When I saw them again, I would ask them if the prayer was making a difference in their daily walk with God. I love to hear when someone says, "It is working for me, and I passed it on to another family member or friend!" This went on for many years, and every day I was expecting something great to happen. My expectancy for the prayer only increased.

I joined my current church in October of 2014. I have an awesome Pastor who operates in excellence and a team based ministry. The only superstar in the church is Jesus Christ! She empowers the members who want to get involve for the Kingdom. Second Sunday is when the poetry ministry have members get up and recite or read a prayer. There was a young lady who stood in front of the church and recited a poem that she had written. At that moment God said enter the prayer to the poetry ministry! The following week on October 7, 2014, I found the Deacon who is over the poetry ministry. I gave him a copy of the prayer, and told him that I would be willing to contribute it to the poetry ministry. A few weeks later, he text me back and said, "Hi Anthony, your poem was well received. We will talk after the anniversary Gala. Please be patient. We only present on the second Sunday." A couple of months went by, and he approached me at a Men's Ministry meeting on Monday and told me that the coming Sunday, December 14, 2014, he wanted me to present the poem in front of the church. He said I know it is short notice, but can you do it. I told him that my wife and I have been saying this prayer everyday for years!! When I told him my wife and I had been saying it together, he told me it would be even better for us to recite it together. We both stood up in front of the congregation for both services, and recited the prayer. The prayer lined up with the message that our Pastor delivered which was about giving. I never lost my expectancy. It took four years after I put it on paper for something significant to happen, but it happened. This book is based off of the same prayer. The message here is many times we are expecting things like money and other material things to come to us. However, God is about Kingdom business. God knows your heart, and will test your expectancy in the little things before he can take you to a higher level.

Remember, God is the author. I want you to expect that your time is coming. We have to understand that God is never late and he does not make mistakes. Having expectancy daily with a great attitude will allow God to work through you. When your time is coming, it will not always be easy. Satan wants you to give up on your dreams.

The devil wants to always keep you down. John 10:10 says, "The thief comes to steal and kill and destroy. I came that they may have life and have it abundantly." Jesus wants you to keep your hope, and know that Satan cannot put more on you than you can handle. Jesus will not allow him. We have to constantly expect that any situation we go through, we will come out of it on top. Remember, spring always comes after winter. You may be going through a storm right now, but hang in there and don't complain. When you expect to come out of it better than before, God will deliver for you. Take time on your own to read the book of Job in the Bible. He was expecting God's best and that is what he eventually got.

I do not want you to get the impression that you will always have to wait a long time for positive things to happen for you. Expect to advance faster. You may have been hoping and expecting for something that normally will take someone of the world years to do. However, God may be looking to advance you faster. You may be on a job, and in the natural, it may take you years to move up and get promoted because you are not qualified. You could be trying to open a business and advance your business, and it normally may take five to 10 years. However, I believe that God will advance you faster when you have a high level of expectancy from Him. It is also a good idea to ask God for something in prayer the first time, and when you pray about that issue going forward, you need to thank God in advance like it has already happened. For example, ask God to place a hedge of protection around your family. After the first time, say thank you God for placing a hedge of protection around my family. When you put high expectations on what you expect from God, it makes him smile because that means that you trust him and believe in him. Trusting and having hope that God will advance you faster will keep you expecting something great today. Do not get discouraged or bored with your thirst for expecting better. I have set on my phone daily around nine to reimagine my dreams. We have to keep expecting every day that our best is yet to come.

We have been talking about several different examples of expectancy. However, there is one thing that we should be expecting all the time. Jesus is coming back one day soon. Matthew 24:44 says, "Therefore you must be ready, for the Son of Man is coming at an hour you do not expect." Listen; make the commitment today to get better for Christ. We do not know when he is coming back. Many believe they have plenty of occasions to give God time. However, you just read that he is coming at an hour we do not expect!! That means that we need to live with the expectancy of doing more for Jesus Christ daily. Live your life daily with doing your best for God. It may be studying the Bible daily, doing something good for someone in need, or praising God every chance you get and letting Jesus know how much you love him.

The last bit of expectancy that we need to have is eternal life. John 3:16 says, "For God so loved the world that he gave his only Son, that whosoever believes in him shall not perish, but have eternal life." We are all here for a temporary amount of time. However, when you are a child of the Almighty God, you have an expectancy of eternal life. Commit yourself to doing God's will after you confess that Jesus is Lord (Romans 10:9).

What do you need to do to increase your expectancy? First, you have to have hope and believe that Jesus Christ is Lord. Expect that God will come through for you, and be patient. Have faith that God is working behind the scenes to advance you faster. I want you to also pray this prayer:

Lord you said in Jeremiah 29:11, "For I know the plans I have for you, declares the Lord, plans for welfare and not for evil, to give you a future and a hope." Lord I trust you and expect that you will advance me further faster. Lord, I expect that you will give me the desires of my heart to help advance the kingdom of God. Continue to give me the thirst to expect greatness from you today. In Jesus Name, Amen.

INCREASE MY SANITY

THE DEFINITION OF sanity is the ability to think and behave in a normal and rational manner; sound mental health. God put increasing my sanity on my heart because of the words sound mental health. We have a tendency at times to let the pressures of life keep us down. When our spiritual mentality is strong we will be able to deal with anything.

I want to also explain the definition of insanity. The definition of insanity is doing the same thing over and over again and expecting different results. I am not trying to call anyone insane. However, when we do not turn to Jesus and expect things to turn out differently, we are making a mistake. We often turn to worldly things and believe that these worldly things will satisfy all of our needs. These things may satisfy us for a short time, but eventually we will lose interest because those things will not give us unconditional satisfaction.

Daily we should have the mentality that we are going to do good for someone when the opportunity presents itself. I cannot express enough that transforming our mind is the key to having sound mental health. I found when I focus on God day and night, my day is smoother, and my problems are at a minimum. Notice I did not say I do not have any problems. Everyday some challenges comes up. However, since I have scripture in me, and I know God is guiding my steps, I know that God causes me to triumph.

We should not let our fears take over us. 2 Timothy 1:7 says, "For God gave us a spirit not of fear but of power and love and self-control." Get rid of low self esteem and an "I can't do it" spirit. We have to wake up every morning with positive feelings. We have to know that we can do anything we put our minds to as long as we put God first. We go to Jesus with everything and he will give us confirmation when what we are asking for is His will for our life.

So how do we increase our sanity? We increase our sanity by transforming our self-centered mind into a spiritual and righteousness Christ-like mind. This takes discipline and training from the Holy Spirit. We also need to stay in the word of God to give our minds strength. I want you to also pray this prayer:

Lord Jesus, 2 Timothy 3:16 says, "All scripture is breathed out by God and profitable for teaching for reproof, and training in righteousness." Help me to transform my mind so I can think more Christ like to become the righteousness of God. In Jesus Name, Amen.

I cannot stress enough that you need to change the way you think to get the results you are looking for. Do not get discouraged or have a negative mindset because God cannot use you. Stay positive and Jesus will guide you to becoming victorious!!

INCREASE MY BLESSINGS

ONE DEFINITION OF the word blessing is to praise, congratulate, or salute. Another definition is God's favor and protection. A blessing is something that everyone wants. James 1:17 states, "Every good gift is from above, coming down from the Father of lights with whom there is no variation or shadow due to change." There are different ways to get blessings. However, the one that I have found that works the best for me is when I become a blessing for someone else. We should go out of our way to help someone in need and to just be kind to someone daily. No matter what circumstance you are in, you can always help someone. Do not get down on yourself and say I am having such a tough time right now. Instead think about who needs help that you can impact today.

Most of us have heard the saying "when praises go up, blessing come down." Look to give encouraging words to someone every day. It may be a compliment. I like that suite you have on or I like those shoes you are wearing. When we honor others, God will honor us. This is huge when it comes to receiving blessings!! I like to look at it as every time you do something nice for someone, a huge bucket in heaven will get water (blessings) poured in it. Once you do enough good things for people or towards people, the bucket will overflow and the blessings will come down to you from heaven. It is a repeat cycle. When you constantly are being good to people with kind words and actions, the blessing will come down. Once they come down, you keep blessing someone else. Some of you are saying, "I am good to people, and nothing is happening. I do not see any blessings." Can I tell you something? First, you are seeing yourself doing a good deed for someone else. Second, God does not always make things happen the next day. Those blessings are coming. You just need to stay obedient and watch God begin to bless you.

Giving is another way to see blessings. Luke 6:38 says, "Give, and it will be given to you. Good measure, pressed down, shaken together, running over, will be put into your lap. For with the measure you use it will be measured back to you." We often associate giving with money. Money is good to give. However, giving is also your time. Volunteer to serve in one of the ministries that your church has. Find your fit, and serve where you are comfortable. I have learned that when you are serving in an area that is natural to you, more than likely that is your fit. For example, I love to encourage and mentor people so I joined the Pastoral Care ministry at my church. This is a ministry that helps members that are going through bereavement and other difficult times. This is when people need encouragement and to let them know God is in control. He will see them through the situation and we are here to help. This makes me feel enthusiastic because it is something I enjoy. I expressed to you in the finance chapter that God loves a cheerful giver. In this chapter I just told you that for the measure you use it will be measured back to you. When you give your time or money, give it cheerfully. God is looking at your enthusiasm and dedication to what you are doing. He knows our heart. When we are not giving it our all, this is the measure we will get back. We should all want the best out of our lives. This is how we get it by giving maximum effort in what we do. This does work. I have been giving my best in my tithing, and God has been blessing me. I have been giving my best effort when it comes to attending church, bible study, and other ministries in the church, and God has been blessing my family because of the effort and faith. I have seen people attend church on Sunday, but do not get involved in anything else for the ministry. When you have to work or something else comes up, it is understandable. Even when you need to spend quality home time because the family has been doing a lot of running around, and have not spent time together. However, if you are not making the attempt to get involved because you just want to stay home, that is not giving God your best. We have to give God our best effort. He knows that you get tired sometimes, but he wants to see how much effort you are going to make to serve him even when it gets rough. You serve the company you work for by getting to work on time (I hope you get there on time), but you do not get to church on time. I do not understand it!! God made the job you have, and yet we will honor the job more than him. I do not get it. I am not judging, and if it doesn't apply to your life that is good. However, if I just got under your skin, it may be because you know you could do better. Give God your best effort so he can take care of you with a shower of blessings.

The next thing that we need to do, is give God more praise and worship. Start to just thank him for waking you up every morning. Thank him for your family, and thank him for dying on the cross for your sins. God loves those praises that you give him. Tell him how awesome and magnificent he is. Stay in constant conversation with him. Every opportunity I have during the day, I sometime just simply say, "Thank you Lord for being my Father." God will shower down blessings when you boast about him and let him know he is the best. I know in this world that when you give some people praise that they have a tendency to get full of themselves, and sometime do not appreciate the respect and praise that you give them. However, with God you do not have to worry about looking as if you are kissing up to people. The Lord ALMIGHTY is the only one that you can give all the praise and glory, and he does not give you any negative feedback.

Let me tell you something. Your time is coming. Do not worry about the blessings not happening fast enough. Think of it like making deposits into the stock market. You will not always see gains every day. However, when you keep depositing in the market, you will eventually see some gains in due time. It could not be simply the right time for you to receive certain blessings. However, with patience God will give you blessings. You know how you buy something and there is a trial period? That is how it is with our blessings. God will not always give you a blessing for something that you do right away. Pass the test and do not grumble and complain when the blessing is not coming fast enough for you. Wait on the Lord because the blessing is on the way. Psalm 84:11 says, "For the Lord God is sun and shield; the Lord bestows favor and honor. No good thing does he withhold from those who walk uprightly." Uprightly is meaning in this case being the Righteousness of God. Doing the things God has commanded us to do will get us the blessings we want and deserve.

Have a servant heart. It is an honor to serve people. I know that society will try and make us believe that being a servant is a bad thing. Think for just one moment about going to a restaurant today. In the past, remember the waiter or waitress use to come to your table and say, "welcome to this restaurant. My name is Anthony, and I will be your server today." Notice how the greeting is in most restaurants today. "Welcome to this restaurant. My name is Anthony, and I will be taking care of you today!" Our society has made the word servant a distasteful word. John 12:26 says, "If anyone serves me, he must follow me; and where I am, there will my servant be also. If anyone serves me, the Father will honor him." We have to have a willing heart to serve. When you have a willing heart to serve it makes serving pleasurable. This will show God how much you love him, and it will line you up for your blessings.

There is another area that God has put on my heart to share so we can enter into a season of blessings. We have to make serving others, being kind to someone daily, and complimenting (honoring) each other daily a lifestyle. Some of us like to work out, and it has become a part of our daily life. These areas mentioned have to become your daily passion. Go out of your way to make someone's life better today. If you come in contact with people that are speaking negative about someone, find something positive to say in that situation. Start practicing this today, and see how God will make you a blessing for someone else.

How can you increase your blessing? Start by being a blessing for someone else. We have to make a conscious effort daily to do something kind for someone else. It could be as simple as giving everyone you see a compliment for the day, Praise God for all he has done for you, what he is doing for you now, and will continue to do for you in the future. I want you to also pray this prayer:

Jesus, your word says in James 1:17 "Every good gift and every perfect gift is from above, coming down from the Father of lights with whom there is no variation or shadow due to change." Lord,

continue to shower my family with blessings. Allow me to be a blessing to someone else, and have a willing and servant heart to let your light shine through me to them today. In Jesus Name, Amen

Thank him every opportunity that you have. Make it your daily business to have a willing servant heart. Commit an act of kindness to people you come in contact with. Learn how to be patient and wait on the blessing. Remember, it does not always happen when we want it, but God is always on time. Continue to be obedient and faithful to his word, and God will bless you in numerous ways. Remember, you can become the blessing for others.

INCREASE MY FAVOR

THE DEFINITION OF favor is an attitude of approval or liking. Key word in this definition is attitude. When we deal with God, he is examining us to see how we will respond to everything that is put before us. Favor is something that we long for. We all need a little help to thrust us to the next level. As an Army JROTC Instructor, within the first week of the school year, I like to show a video about Colin Powell. He is a retired four star general and went on to become secretary of state. Colin Powell has done many great things. On the video, he talks about how he started out mopping floors in a Pepsi-Cola plant. He told how day after day he mopped the floors the best way he knew how. One day, a supervisor told him that he noticed how he was mopping the floors, and he wanted to give him a promotion. The message was that do the best job all the time because someone is always looking. When you think no one is paying attention to the little things someone will notice you when you are doing your best.

God wants us to have a spirit of excellence. We have to ask God to make us aware of giving our best. It starts in our thinking. Get a plan and goal on where you want to see yourself this time next year. Now, start working towards it. Psalms 5:12 states, "For you bless the righteous, O Lord; you cover him with favor as with the shield." God blesses the righteous with favor. Ladies and gentlemen, like I have said many times before in this book, it starts with the little things. When I committed to living a life of excellence, I made up in my mind that the little things that I may have ignored before, I would start taking action and holding myself accountable. For example, walking around the school grounds, I use to see trash in my path on the way to the administration's office. I use to ignore it and think someone else will get it. I have now committed to picking it up and putting it in the trash myself. How can I live in excellence looking the other way when I know I can do better? Keep in mind that I do not go around the whole campus picking up trash. God wants us to commit to excellence the things he puts in our path. I want the best of what God has to offer me, and I understand that having a spirit of excellence is the only way that I am going to get the best that Jesus has for me. I want to be better for God. It is not about me, but being a better ambassador for Christ. Yes, this takes more effort. However, God will show you that he is having favor on your life when you commit to this. Do not be lazy. Make an outline of the things that you want to be better at from this day forward. Pray to God to make you aware of the things you have committed to, and help you to operate in excellence. Operating in excellence will take faith and a willing heart to be obedient. It will not be easy to do this alone. However, God will be with you every step of the way. God does see your faith and obedience to him, and he will grant you favor.

When everyone around you may not be committing to excellence, do not let that stop you. God is in control and will exalt you for your effort to do your best. Genesis 6: 5-9 says, "The Lord saw how great the wickedness of the human race had become on the earth, and that every inclination of the thoughts of the human heart was only evil all the time. The Lord regretted that he had made human beings on the earth, and his heart was deeply troubled. So the Lord said, "I will wipe from the face of the earth the human race I have created—and with them the animals, the birds and the creatures that move along the ground-for I regret that I have made them. But Noah found favor in the eyes of the Lord. This is the account of Noah and his family. Noah was a righteous man, blameless among the people of his time, and he walked faithfully with God." Notice that God found favor with Noah because he was a righteous man who walked faithfully with God. He was the only one that did not live with wickedness in his heart. We have to stand alone if we want God's best. Even when everyone else around us is not being righteous, you have to operate in excellence. Can it be lonely? Yes and No. People will start to distance themselves from you because of your commitment to doing the right thing. Hebrews 10:25 states, " Not forsaking the assembling of ourselves together, as the manner of some is; but exhorting one another; and so much the more, as ye see the day approaching." I put this in here because this scripture is talking about fellowship with our fellow Christians which is a good thing. When you are seeking the kingdom of God first and operating in excellence, not everyone will be happy for you. Some may see the anointing on your life and get jealous. We hope that other believers will embrace the goodness that God has for you, but remember that we are human. Pray for them that God will not harden their hearts. However, you have to keep operating in excellence. Luke 2:52 states, "And Jesus increased in wisdom and in stature and in favor with God and man." God will send you new Christian friends that have the same desires you have. Remember, Jesus is with you every step of the way so you will not be lonely. Noah found favor when everyone else was not trying to do right. You do not have to make an announcement that you are operating in excellence and I can't hang around you guys anymore!! Keep running your race and let God do the rest.

Have faith and believe that favor is coming. Psalm 102:13 says, "You will arise and have pity on Zion; it is the time to favor her; the appointed time has come." Your season of favor may have not come in your past. That is because that time is already set. God is still on the throne. He does not make any mistakes. Everything is perfectly orchestrated for you to win and triumph (read 2 Corinthians 2:14). We have to not get discouraged and keep our faith strong so that when favor shows up, we are ready to receive it. We should not be down and complaining talking about it will never happen for me. I guess I missed my chance at favor, Anthony, I am getting to old; God can't use me! We will not be available to receive it with our body and soul polluted with these thoughts. Operating in excellence is keeping a good attitude that we need to win.

When favor does come upon you, you will get a chance to see what the people that are closest to you are really about. Are they for you or are they against you? Their true colors will come out. All I want to tell you here is remember that you are not looking for approval or to please man. God is the only one that you need to please. Do not look for favor from man. Colossians 3:23-24 states, "Whatever you do, work heartily, as for the Lord and not for men, knowing that from the Lord you will receive the inheritance as your reward. You are serving the Lord Christ." If people give you accolades, accept it humbly and give God all the glory. However, if it does not happen, shake your boots off and move on. Your future is too great to let someone or something hold you back.

How do you increase your favor? Operate, Operate, Operate in excellence. We have to start doing our best in everything that we do. When we volunteer and we are not getting paid to do something, we have to still do our best. When we think we are not being watched, remember Jesus is always watching. I want you to also pray this prayer:

> **Lord, you said in Genesis 18:3, "O Lord, if I have found favor in your sight, do not pass by your servant." Jesus, I know that these were Abraham's words. However, Lord I want you to find favor in me Lord. Help me to operate in the spirit of excellence so that I will find abundant favor with you. Guide my mind, body, and spirit to do your will and have a willing heart to do my best every day to represent you. In Jesus Name, Amen.**

LORD, THE BATTLE IS NOT MINE, IT'S YOURS

THE DEFINITION OF battle is a sustained fight between large, organized armed forces. There is a battle going on every day that you are involved in. It is called spiritual warfare. God's Armor protects us (Christians) against spiritual forces of evil in this world. Ephesians 6:13-18 describes the spiritual armor God gives us. It says, "Therefore put on the full armor of God, so that when the day of evil comes, you may be able to stand your ground, and after you have done everything, to stand. Stand firm then, with the belt of truth buckled around your waist, with the breastplate of righteousness in place, and with your feet fitted with the readiness that comes from the gospel of peace. In addition to all this, take up the shield of faith, with which you can extinguish all the flaming arrows of the evil one. Take the helmet of salvation and the sword of the Spirit, which is the word of God. And pray in the Spirit on all kinds of prayers and requests. With this in mind, be alert and always keep on praying for all the Lord's people." We can win all of these battles when we have a relationship with Jesus Christ. It is only through Jesus Christ that Christians have any power over Satan and his demons. That is why we should rebuke Satan in the name of Jesus.

Once you have given your life to Christ, stop trying to fight these battles on your own. God has promised us several things that will help you fight these battles. God has promised that his grace is sufficient for the Christians. 2 Corinthians 12:9 says, "Be he said to me, "My grace is sufficient for you, for my power is made perfect in weakness. "Therefore I will boast all the more gladly about my weaknesses, so that Christ's power may rest on me." We gain grace by our faith. Romans 5:2 say, "Through whom we have gained access by faith into his grace in which we now stand. And we boast in the hope of the glory of God." When things get tough in this battle throughout your life, remember the promise that God's grace is sufficient. Do not get discouraged.

God has promised to supply all of our needs. Philippians 4:19 says, "But my God shall supply all your needs according to his riches in glory by Christ Jesus." God has promised all of our needs not all of our wants. Stop worrying about having food and a place to live. He has promised those things for those who believe and have faith in him. If he gives you some of your wants, that is great. However, knowing that you have everything you need will keep you at peace.

God has promised that his children will not be overtaken by temptation. Satan is the one that tempts us, and God will test us. God has promised us a way of escape. 1 Corinthians 10:13 states, "No temptation has overtaken you that is not common to man. God is faithful, and he will not let you be tempted beyond your ability, but with the temptation he will also provide the way of escape, that you may be able to endure it." Once we are a child of God, any temptation that comes our way we can get out of it. Whether it is lust, greed, gluttony, envy, pride, anger, sloth, or any other sin, you can overcome it. That is a battle that we can win once we realize we are being tempted. Think about your weaknesses and be on guard from this day forward.

God has promised us victory over death. Jesus gave his life as a ransom for our sins. 1 Corinthians 15:57 says, "But thanks be to God! He gives us the victory through our Lord Jesus Christ." Once you confess with your mouth that Jesus is Lord you are saved and have victory over death. Romans 10:9-10 states, "If you declare with your mouth, "Jesus is Lord," and believe in your heart that God raised him from the dead, you will be saved. For it is with your heart that you believe and are justified, and it is with your mouth that you profess your faith and are saved." Get your victory over death by making Jesus Christ your Lord and Savior.

God has also promised that those that believe in Jesus and are baptized for the forgiveness of sins will be saved. Mark 16:16 says, "Whoever believes and is baptized will be saved, but whoever does not believe will be condemned." Enough said.

God has promised that all things worked together for good to those who love and serve him faithfully. Romans 8:28 says, "And we know that in all things God works for the good of those who love him, who have been called to his purpose." When we have times of bereavement and difficult times in life we do not always see this. When I was laid off from my job, I was thinking to myself, I was faithful, how could this happen to me? I was trying to do everything I could to get a job as soon as possible, but God did not allow it to happen. He supplied all my needs like he promised. I did not fall behind on any bills. As I lost my job, my wife was offered a position that made the amount of money I was making at the school so we were able to maintain. When I did all I could do, I just had to kneel and ask God for guidance. During the six months I was unemployed, I begin to develop a more intimate relationship with God. I made a commitment to read and study my Bible daily. My walk with God became stronger. He restored me in a year. I did not see it at the time, but it all worked for my good because of a stronger walk with God. When we are going through difficult times, have faith that God is preparing something better for you in the future. Trust him when you cannot see a light at the end of the tunnel, know that he is the light of the world.

Finally, God has promised Christians eternal life. John 10:27-28 states, "My sheep listen to my voice; I know them, and they follow me. I give them eternal life, and they shall never perish; no one will snatch them out of my hand." It does feel peaceful to know as Christians, when we leave this life which is temporary, we will live in heaven for Eternity. I want you to also pray this prayer:

Lord, 2 Chronicles 20:15 says, "He said: Listen, King Jehoshaphat and all who live in Judah and Jerusalem! This is what the Lord says to you: Do not be afraid or discouraged because of this vast army. For the battle is not yours, but God's." Jesus, help me to understand that I am in a battle of spiritual warfare. I demand that you make me spiritually equip to be victorious in all battles! Place a hedge of protection around my family and keep us away from evil. Help me to realize and understand all the promises

you have given me and to live by them. Help me to understand that I have an escape plan for all temptation and that all things work for my good because I am faithful and love you Jesus. I will win and triumph because of you. Instead of getting down, I will praise you and honor you in my time of trouble. Thank you for eternal life. In Jesus name, Amen.

MY HARVEST IS ON THE WAY

THE DEFINITION OF harvest is the process or period of gathering in crops. There is a timeframe in between the time we plant a seed until it actually bears fruit. When a farmer plants a seed, he waits until the estimated timeframe for the crop to become ripe. The difference between the wait we have as Christians from the wait the farmer has is that we have to be patient and obedient to see our harvest come into fruition without knowing exactly when it is coming. I can give you an example from my life. A seed was planted in me for salvation at the Baptist church I grew up in Philadelphia, PA. After being sidetracked for many years and conforming to this world, I rededicated my life to Christ. The seed was watered and started to grow at a church called Bethel AME Kissimmee. I loved my time at that church. However, in the beginning of 2014, God told me it was time to move on. In August of 2014, I found a church that I could feel the Holy Spirit moving inside of me. In October of 2014, I joined Majestic Life Church in Orlando where I am currently still a member of the body of Christ. This is where I am seeing my harvest start to come into fruition. I love the team based ministry, and my family is also growing more than I have seen in the past. It has been 30 years since I have given my life to the Lord, and now my harvest is on the way. This is the most obedient and faithful that I have ever been to God. I now see what being faithful and obedient to God will get you. I am at peace in all areas of my life. I am not saying that everything is roses. There are always trials of this life. However, I am now equipped to recognize them. I know how to deal with them and I make better decision because I keep Jesus as my first priority in life. Through it all I did not lose hope of a better life. I kept believing and dreaming that things would get better, and now I am going to leave my mark on this generation.

I cannot tell you what is on the way for you. However, I can tell you that as a Christian, your reward for your obedience and faith goes beyond this world. This is a deep chapter so please stay with me. It is worth reading several times to reinforce that your harvest is on the way.

Let us start from the beginning. Jesus died on the cross for our sins. When we confess with our mouths that Jesus is Lord, and believe in your heart that God raised him from the dead, then we are saved. When Jesus Christ returns, we will face judgment. Judgment is not for our sins, which we are washed clean by the blood of Christ on the cross, but judgment will be for our works here on Earth. We will be held liable for the actions or deeds we carried out in our daily lives. Our eternal destiny is by no means an issue (since you are a Christian). However, the scope and size of our reward is in question. 2 Corinthians 5:10 says, "For we must all stand before Christ to be judged. We will each receive whatever we deserve for the good or evil we have done in this earthly body," So that is why the scripture also says judge not or you will be judged. Judgment is reserved for Jesus Christ.

As it is here on earth, when we get to heaven, we will not all have the same status. Matthew 19:30 says, "But as many who seem to be important now will be the least important then, and those who are considered least here will be great then." God loves us all forever, but some will be given positions of higher power, class, and responsibility than others. What we do here on earth will determine our status in heaven. If we just sit in church, and do not make an effort to serve in the ministry we may get minimal responsibility in heaven. Heaven will be a place where true integrity will have supremacy.

Let us talk about the eternal treasures in heaven. The ultimate treasure is of course eternal life. You can have treasure in heaven beyond eternal life. Compare it to an athlete that makes it to the pros. Why don't all of them become all-stars? It is because the all-stars work harder to be the best, and some of the players are just happy to be there. Jesus does not want us to fixate our minds on the treasures of this world because he knows that they will go away. Matthew 6:19-21 says, "Do not store up treasures here on earth, where moths eat them and rust destroys them, and where thieves break in and steal. Store your treasures in heaven, where moths and rust cannot destroy, and thieves do not break in and steal. Wherever your treasure is, there the desire of your heart will also be." These things here on earth are only temporary. Yet, we spend most of our lives trying to obtain the fancy cars, mansions, etc. What God has for us in heaven is better than anything that we can imagine. 1 Corinthians 2:9 says, "However, as it is written: "What no eye has seen, what no ear has heard, and no human mind has conceived" the things God has prepared for those who love him."

Some of us may never live in a mansion here on earth. Do not worry. As a Christian, we have a heavenly mansion prepared by Jesus that we do not have to worry about a mortgage, and all the other nuisances that come along with the mansions of this world. In John 14 Jesus is talking to the disciples. John 14:1-3 states, "Do not let your hearts be troubled. You believe in God, believe in me. My Father's house has many dwelling places (homes). If it were not so, I would have told you; for I am going away to prepare a place for you. And when I go and make ready a place for you, I will come back again and will take you to myself, that where I am you may be also."

Jesus will award us with crowns. The belief in Jesus is just the beginning. Jesus is the foundation, and we are to build a collection of works that profit the Lord. Like I told you before, not one of these works is required for our salvation, but if we really trust in him, it will be our satisfaction to carry out such good deeds. There are five crowns that the bible mentions. Let us talk about the crowns that you will receive when you put in the work for God Almighty!!

Crown of Rejoicing. There are two specific scriptures that talk about the crown of rejoicing. 1 Thessalonians 2:19-20 says, "For what is our hope or happiness or our victor's wreath of exultant triumph when we stand in the presence of our Lord Jesus at his coming? Is it not you? For you are (indeed) our glory and our joy!" The other is Philippians 4:1. It states, "Therefore, my brothers, you whom I love and long for, my joy and crown, that is how you should stand firm in the Lord, dear friends!" This crown is held in reserve for those whose hard work have led to others becoming believers in Jesus Christ.

The crown will be a source of pride and joy for all eternity. If you want this crown, make sure to share the gospel of Jesus with others every time God presents an opportunity.

Crown of Victory. 1 Corinthians 9:25 says, "Everyone who competes in the games goes into strict training. They do it to get a crown that will not last, but we do it to get a crown that will last forever." This crown is set aside for those who, through cautious obedience, have triumph over the desires of the flesh. Through means of the Holy Spirit, they managed to progressively disengage themselves from the control of the temptations of this world. If you want to win this crown, make sure to pay attention to and stand by the Holy Spirit within you. Coach yourself so that every reflection, emotion, and deed is considered and judged in accordance to God's will for your life.

Crown of Righteousness. 2 Timothy 4:8 states, "And now the prize awaits me- the crown of righteousness, which the Lord, the righteous Judge will give me on the day of his return. And the prize is not just for me but for all who eagerly look forward to his appearing." The verse actually says what it is for. This one is set aside for those who eagerly await the return of Jesus Christ. If you want to win this crown, live every day with the continuous anticipation that Christ could come back at any moment.

Crown of Life. There are two scriptures in the bible that refer to the crown of life. First is Revelation 2:10. It says, "Don't be afraid of what you are about to suffer. The devil will throw some of you into prison to test you. You will suffer for ten days. But if you remain faithful even when facing death, I will give you the crown of life." It is also in James 1:12. It states, "God blesses those who patiently endure testing and temptation. Afterward they will receive the crown of life that God has promised to those who love him." This crown is set aside for those who endure temptation, suffering, persecution, and testing for Jesus Christ. If you want this crown, love Jesus Christ more than anything. Love him more than your own life.

Crown of Glory. 1 Peter 5:1-4 says, "And now, a word to you who are elders in the churches. I, too, am an elder and a witness to the sufferings of Christ. And I, too, will share in his glory when he is revealed to the whole world. As a fellow elder, I appeal to you: care for the flock that God has entrusted to you. Watch over it willingly, not grudgingly-not for what you will get out of it, but because you are eager to serve God. Don't lord it over the people assigned to your care, but lead them by your own good example. And when the Great Shepherd appears, you will receive a crown of never-ending glory and honor." This crown is set aside for those who are placed in a position of authority and accountability in earthly life. Others will be looking to us for us to lead by example. This is a task of gigantic importance. These leaders must show love and be humble. They must cautiously watch over those with whom they have been assigned. Their intentions and hearts must be wholesome. They must focus on God rather than making the center of attention on themselves. If you want to win this crown, make sure to be a fine illustration to others, particularly those looking to you for direction. Also, be a superior and truthful steward of those God has entrusted to your care.

Your harvest will be on the way if you continue to be obedient, faithful and patient. I do not want you to think that the only harvest you will receive is when you get to heaven. That is not the message I am trying to send here. There will be a harvest here on earth for you that is temporary. Enjoy them in the moment. However, isn't it satisfying to know that we have the opportunity to receive eternal treasures that will last for all eternity? I do not know about you, but eternity sounds a lot longer than 70, 80, or 90 years!! If you have not already been doing it, start storing up those treasures in heaven. I can only imagine the mansion and the crowns we will have. I can only imagine standing before Jesus casting my crown at his feet. I can only imagine my status in heaven because of my deeds that I am performing to advance the kingdom of God. The question I want to ask you today is; what are you doing to reap your harvest? Operate in excellence, and get your best harvest out of your life.

FINAL THOUGHTS

GOD HAS RESERVED your destiny for you, and no one can take that away. We all have a different journey to fulfill his purpose for our lives. This is the reason that God has made you unique. I want you to understand that his thoughts are not our thoughts. Although it may be hard to understand on our level of thinking, but his thinking is far more superior to ours.

From this day forward, make a commitment daily to follow these principles in this book to witness increase in your life. All of these principles work, but the only way to find out, is to put them in action. God wants you to be victorious. He does not want you to be defeated by the enemy.

Have a willing heart to serve God in everything that you do. God is not going to force you to do anything. God is a gentlemen, and he does not want you to feel obligated to do his will. God wants you to feel excited and cheerful to serve him. Think about children when they are at an age where they enjoy coloring and making pictures for their parents. They have a willing heart because they want to show you that they love you. They want to do the right thing because they want you to be proud of them. Get into that mindset with Jesus. Serve him with a willing heart because you want to show him how much you love him. Human approval should not be your focus. Show yourself worthy to the Lord. That is what matters.

Do not become a pretender of faith. Do not be a person that says they are a Christian, but their actions show something different. I want you to understand that this walk with God is not easy. However, God is in total control. The devil can only tempt you with God's approval. Some of you may wonder why God allows it to happen to me. He allows it to happen to see if when times are hard you really love him. It is easy to enjoy things when everything is going good. However, when adversity strikes, that is when you find a person's true character. God is testing your faith and seeing what you are made of when the chips are down. Stay strong and fight the good fight of faith.

You cannot do this alone. If it was that easy, you would not need Jesus. God has designed everything so that it comes back to depending on him, and that is ok. That is how he wants it to be. His plan for your life has already been determined. We have to line up our life with faith, obedience, trust, and a willing heart to find out our destiny. When you are operating in excellence, he will start to open the doors on that pathway to greatness. I do not care if you have $10 in your bank account or 1 billion dollars in the account. Operating in excellence will help you get to the next level in glory along with being consistent and patient.

Take time to help someone else, and make their lives better. We are not supposed to accumulate an abundance of things and just keep everything to ourselves. That is what the world teaches us, but that is not what God wants us to do. Give back to your community and help those in need. It will give you a peace of mind. Understand that the battle is not yours, it is the Lord's. Spiritual Warfare goes on every day, and God has equipped us with spiritual armor. Lastly, remember that your harvest is on the way. Do not give up, and you will see some of your earthly harvest, but more importantly you will see your eternal harvest one day. Everyone that you plant a seed in for Christ, they will be in heaven due to your good work!

Read and apply the prayers in this book, and the prayer on the back of this book with the principles, and make it a part of your daily lifestyle and passion. Share the principles of this book and the prayer with everyone you come in contact with so you can become a blessing to them. I guarantee God will turn things around in your life and take you to places that are beyond your imagination.